BOOKS BY MONA VAN DUYN

IF IT BE NOT I

COLLECTED POEMS
1959-1982

IF IT BE NOT I

COLLECTED POEMS
1959-1982

Mona Van Duyn

ALFRED A. KNOPF

New York

1993

THIS IS A BORZOI BOOK
PUBLISHED BY ALFRED A. KNOPF, INC.

Merciful Disguises, copyright © 1966, 1968, 1969, 1970, 1971, 1972, 1973 by
Mona Van Duyn

Letters from a Father and Other Poems, copyright © 1982 by Mona Van Duyn

Poems from *Merciful Disguises* appeared in the following previously published books:

VALENTINES TO THE WIDE WORLD: copyright 1942, 1944, 1953, 1954, © 1956, 1957, 1958, 1959 by Mona Van Duyn
A TIME OF BEES: copyright © 1960, 1962, 1963, 1964 by Mona Van Duyn
TO SEE, TO TAKE: copyright © 1964, 1965, 1966, 1967, 1968, 1969, 1970, 1971 by Mona Van Duyn
BEDTIME STORIES: copyright © 1972, 1973 by Mona Van Duyn

New poems from *Merciful Disguises* originally appeared in:

COUNTER/MEASURES, THE NEW AMERICAN REVIEW, THE NEW REPUBLIC, THE NEW YORKER, THE OHIO REVIEW, PEBBLE, POETRY, THE POETRY BAG, THE QUARTERLY REVIEW OF LITERATURE and STRIVER'S ROW

Poems from *Letters from a Father and Other Poems* originally appeared in:

AMERICAN POETRY REVIEW, COUNTER/MEASURES, CROSSCOUNTRY, THE GEORGIA REVIEW, THE LITTLE MAGAZINE, THE MASSACHUSETTS REVIEW, MICHIGAN QUARTERLY REVIEW, THE NEW YORKER, PLOUGHSHARES, POETRY, POETRY NOW, THE POMEGRANATE PRESS, RIVER STYX, ST. LOUIS LITERARY SUPPLEMENT, THE YALE REVIEW

Library of Congress Cataloging-in-Publication Data

Van Duyn, Mona.
    If it be not I : collected poems, 1959–1982 / Mona Van Duyn.
1st ed.
        p. cm.
    ISBN 0–679–41902–0
    I. Title.
PS3543.A563A6   1993   92–11335
811'.54—dc20   CIP

Manufactured in the United States of America
First Edition

For Jarvis

There was a little woman,
  As I have heard tell,
She went to market
  Her eggs for to sell;
She went to market
  All on a market day,
And she fell asleep
  On the king's highway.

There came by a pedlar,
  His name was Stout,
He cut her petticoats
  All round about;
He cut her petticoats
  Up to her knees;
Which made the little woman
  To shiver and sneeze.

But if this be I,
  As I do hope it be,
I have a little dog at home
  And he knows me;
If it be I,
  He'll wag his little tail,
And if it be not I
  He'll loudly bark and wail!

When this little woman
  Began to awake,
She began to shiver,
  And she began to shake;
She began to shake,
  And she began to cry,
Lawk a mercy on me,
  This is none of I!

Home went the little woman
  All in the dark,
Up starts the little dog,
  And he began to bark;
He began to bark,
  And she began to cry,
Lawk a mercy on me,
  This is none of I!

OLD NURSERY RHYME

CONTENTS

Contents

TO SEE, TO TAKE 1970

BEDTIME STORIES 1972

POEMS 1965–1973

Contents

LETTERS FROM A FATHER, AND OTHER POEMS 1982

LAST

THERE

HERE

FIRST

VALENTINES
TO THE
WIDE WORLD
1959

THREE VALENTINES TO THE WIDE WORLD

I

The child disturbs our view. Tow-head bent, she
stands on one leg and folds up the other. She is listening
to the sound of her fingernail on a scab on her knee.
If I were her mother I would think right now of the chastening
that ridiculous arrangement of bones and bumps must go through,
and that big ear too, till they learn what to do and hear.
People don't perch like something seen in a zoo
or in tropical sections of Florida. They'll have to buy her
a cheap violin if she wants to make scraping noises.
She is eight years old. What in the world could she wear
that would cover her hinges and disproportions? Her face is
pointed and blank, the brows as light as the hair.

"Mother, is love God's hobby?" At eight you don't even
look up from your scab when you ask it. A kid's squeak,
is that a fit instrument for such a question?
Eight times the seasons turned and cold snow tricked
the earth to death, and still she hasn't noticed.
Her friend has a mean Dad, a milkman always kicks
at the dog, but by some childish hocus-pocus
she blinks them away. She counts ten and sucks in her cheeks
and the globe moves under the green thumb of an Amateur,
the morning yelp, the crying at recess are gone.
In the freeness of time He gardens, and to His leisure
old stems entrust new leaves all winter long.

Hating is hard work, and the uncaring thought is hard;
but loving is easy, love is that lovely play
that makes us and keeps us? No one answers you. Such absurd
charity of the imagination has shamed us, Emily.

I remember now. Legs shoved you up, you couldn't tell
where the next tooth would fall out or grow in, or what
your own nose would look like next year. Anything was possible.
Then it slowed down, and you had to keep what you got.
When this child's body stretches to the grace of her notion,
and she's tamed and curled, may she be free enough to bring
mind and heart to that serious recreation
where anything is still possible,—or almost anything.

II

I have never enjoyed those roadside overlooks from which
you can see the mountains of two states. The view keeps
    generating
a kind of pure, meaningless exaltation
that I can't find a use for. It drifts away from things.

And it seems to me also that the truckdriver's waste of the world
is sobering. When he rolls round it on a callous of macadam,
think how all those limping puppydogs, girls
thumbing rides under the hot sun, or under the white moon

how all those couples kissing at the side of the road,
bad hills, cat eyes, and horses asleep on their feet
must run together into a statement so abstract
that it's tiresome. Nothing in particular holds still in it.

Perhaps he does learn that the planet can still support life,
though with some difficulty. Or even that there is injustice,
since he rolls round and round and may be able to feel
the slight but measurable wobble of the earth on its axis.

But what I find most useful is the poem. To find some spot
on the surface and then bear down until the skin can't stand
the tension and breaks under it, breaks under that half-demented
"pressure of speech" the psychiatrists saw in Pound

is a discreetness of consumption that I value. Only the poem
is strong enough to make the initial rupture,
at least for me. Its view is simultaneous
discovery and reminiscence. It starts with the creature

and stays there, assuming creation is worth the time
it takes, from the first day down to the last line on the last page.
And I've never seen anything like it for making you think
that to spend your life on such old premises is a privilege.

III

> *Your yen two wol slee me sodenly;*
> *I may the beautee of hem not sustene.*
> MERCILES BEAUTE

When, in the middle of my life, the earth stalks me
with sticks and stones, I fear its merciless beauty.
This morning a bird woke me with a four-note outcry,
and cried out eighteen times. With the shades down, sleepy
as I was, I recognized his agony.
It resembles ours. With one more heave, the day
sends us a generous orb and lets us see
all sights lost when we lie down finally.

And if, in the middle of her life, some beauty falls on
a girl, who turns under its swarm to astonished woman,
then, into that miraculous buzzing, stung
in the lips and eyes without mercy, strangers may run.
An untended power—I pity her and them.
It is late, late; haste! says the falling moon,
as blinded they stand and smart till the fever's done
and blindly she moves, wearing her furious weapon.

Beauty is merciless and intemperate.
Who, turning this way and that, by day, by night,

still stands in the heart-felt storm of its benefit,
will plead in vain for mercy, or cry, "Put out
the lovely eyes of the world, whose rise and set
move us to death!" And never will temper it,
but against that rage slowly may learn to pit
love and art, which are compassionate.

TWO POEMS, WITH BIRDS

I ADDENDUM TO ANY DAY, ANY POEM

Assume, in a bird's eye, the world as a dainty bulge—
is the problem of definition greater, or less?
In that chipper bubbleful much would be diminished
by restriction, much would mount up to massiveness.
No state of affairs then, but a thousand Affairs of State.
Is this simpler? Or harder? Texture turns into form
if one strolls the hilly bark, or through grassfields, on ground
all mined and thumping with life, hunts bug or stalks worm.

When we eye it, not one bird's worth at a time
but with eyes like zeppelins, it may be the vista bests us,
for what crowds quietly even through snow fence metaphors
is the unexamined life, shifting and lustrous,
and lands may mellow or chill in that weight of particulars.
If our largeness of view leaks, does it let out more
than we mean to waste, minute encounters, tucking,
tipping the day into an imperceptible contour?
Do selves go thin for the fat idea of man,
and think in sackfuls while they drop and scatter
pips, seed, nutmeats, kernels and cores
enough for many a pigeon's simple supper?

II SENTIMENTAL EDUCATION

The North Wind doth blow
and we shall have snow,
and what will the robin do then, poor thing?
He'll sit in the barn
and keep himself warm
and tuck his head under his wing, poor thing.

In summers, graceful as any half-grown bird,
She moved in trees that grew in her own yard,

And flourished there, but on the first schoolday
Down dropped her tears with "I hate History!"

Dead kings and children lay in tidy rows
In the dusty cases of their long-agoes.

But other subjects were lively—even Numbers
Performed at her penciltip its heady wonders,

And Rhyme and Story made such hearty flames
That one by one they singed off all her plumes.

She came down from trees then, and was ready early
All naked to go into love's hurly-burly.

Now she is.grown, and in what winter weathers!
She longs for History, or some such feathers.

One wingful to hide her head would keep her warm—
Or so say the other redbreasts in the barn.

THE GENTLE SNORER

When summer came, we locked up our lives and fled
to the woods in Maine, and pulled up over our heads
a comforter filled with batts of piney dark,
tied with crickets' chirretings and the *bork*
of frogs; we hid in a sleep of strangeness from
the human humdrum.

A pleasant noise the unordered world makes wove
around us. Burrowed, we heard the scud of waves,
wrack of bending branch, or plop of a fish
on his heavy home; the little beasts rummaged the brush.
We dimmed to silence, slipped from the angry pull
of wishes and will.

And then we had a three-weeks cabin guest
who snored; he broke the wilderness of our rest.
As all night long he sipped the succulent air,
that rhythm we shared made visible to the ear
a rich refreshment of the blood. We fed in
unison with him.

A sound we dreamed and woke to, over the snuff
of wind, not loud enough to scare off the roof
the early morning chipmunks. Under our skins
we heard, as after disease, the bright, thin
tick of our time. Sleeping, he mentioned death
and celebrated breath.

He went back home. The water flapped the shore.
A thousand bugs drilled at the darkness. Over
the lake a loon howled. Nothing spoke up for us,
salvagers always of what we have always lost;
and we thought what the night needed was more of man,
he left us so partisan.

FROM YELLOW LAKE: AN INTERVAL

Now in this evening land of fire and shadow,
a swallow world, a fallow world, of lake and meadow,
where the mud turtle flops from his log, flat as our fate,
but the green-headed flies swarm up, so furious is our delight,
and down the red roadway that the sun has gone,
a penitential sparrow drops his dung,
I would peel off my mildewed body like a skin,
but keep my heart, a freshening bloom.
Form upon form, creation seems so near
that separateness fades from the shy vacationer.

Yet however far the frog is adrift in his dream,
his burdening bones are moored in marsh at the edge of the
    stream,
the mole in heavy loam turns his bitter face
from the copulation of beetles who are black as our disgrace,
and the brown spider, an unholy host,
sucks at the throat of the fly, his fainting guest;
for nature suspects this homecoming, and tries
the soft prodigal with his own analogies.

And now the white clouds take a moody lover
as in a cloud the crows, the crows fly over.
Then down from sky, all those dark birds have lit
upon my mind, dear carrion, and feed on it,
since their whole prayer is preying. At the lake's edge
where Darning Needles weave with a secret thread,
in dusk the angler stands and sends from shore,
sweeter than worm or bug, the barbed lure.
Perilously it drops down the deep lake,
where, prismed, moves with watery grace the pike,
who rises, clasps with fangs, his fierce faith,
and drowns in air, his mythos in his mouth;
and questionless bloats out his vacant golden eye,
but his body beats out in carnival agony:

"Fisherman, fisherman, is the love you give
my luck, or is your marvelous luck my love?"

Then from me, over the broken waters, flies a final crow,
and all my questions swell his monstrous craw,
while the bearded owl, who is woods' clumsy oracle,
hoots at the sound of rain, a sleepy miracle.

Now, in this evening land of fire and shadow,
a swallow world, a fallow world, of lake and meadow,
where the mud turtle flops from his log, flat as our fate,
but the green-headed flies swarm up, so furious is our delight,
in my body I would be sleek and dumb
as those white worms, blossoming under their stone—
then, warmed, put on my human clothing and report
back for the wintry work of living, our flawed art,
and conspire in the nailing, brutal and indoors,
that pounds to the poem's shape a summer's metaphors.

DWARF IN THE WOODS

after the paintings of Fred Bliss

If I have been born
my mother was a blue
snake,
and the ground shook
when the blue snake bore me.

The crow's mouth bled
and said, Child,
suck on the root of the wild
cinchona.

I took a pike
of wolfsbane leaf
and went,
bare as the blasted shrub,
to where the bats live.

Bigger than God were the white blossoms,
veined in anger.
I felt the fungus' hands like hunger
at my neck.
Fear fell in a green feather
when the teal
flew over.
Butterflies beat black wings at my head
and under the moth mullein
I hid.

I saw him come,
snuffing the ground.
I heard his teeth
crunch
three white birds.
I felt his breath

and the green branch
broke.

Then the pimpernel began to burn
and spoke,
saying, Son,
you have scratched your right hand on the bramble,
and you will win.

I took my pike.
I heard the words.
And while the tree shed its bitter bark
I fought the wolf in the dark
woods.

INSIGHT

When the car at night
came like a beguiling dog,
its eyes turned and saw
one alley,

surprised and young,
like a girl with her bangs trimmed short.

Nine sparrows on a wire woke,
but gesture of dark and
their Pythagorean number
let them stay.

Exquisitely the kettle slept
and kept
no carnival,
with cheeks the wind forgot as
tambourine.

Across the bricks
on dust
the innocence, surprised and young,
asking what attitude? what origin?
hung
like smell of bread
in a kitchen, baking.

Then the dog
could not stay but turned
away its eyes,
perhaps into very soul
perhaps into other alleys.

3 A. M. IN A WAR YEAR

Then the wise hours, suddenly discovered,
when the bed is a world
and the body covetously remembers.

Objectivity, the stuck balloon, shrivels in hand,
and half of a darkness waits outside
while pictures accumulate between the sheets.

Certain loves are summoned,
certain glances into the earth return,
a few strong phrases excite familiar drums.

Among these presences adjustment
to the resurrection starts and strengths
assemble. Even the tragic clock

hears then each calm cell's recollection
that the body is a process
and it is close to a different day.

WOMAN WAITING

Over the gray, massed blunder of her face
light hung crudely and apologetic sight
crossed in a hurry. Asking very little,
her eyes were patiently placed there.
Dress loved nothing and wandered away
wherever possible, needing its own character.

Used to the stories, we wise children
made pleasant pictures of her when alive, till
someone who knew told us it was never so.

Next, wisely waited to see the hidden dancer,
the expected flare leaping through that fog
of flesh, but no one ever did.
In a last wisdom, conceived of a moment
love lit her like a star and the star burned out.
Interested friends said this had never happened.

NAP

The field tipped over pleasantly and he
snored and returned to death; from there
the back step under his pants grew metaphysical—
its warmth was sin, not sun.

What he remembered next was half-way literal, half true:

The hogs blasphemed creation all the way from home to the
  Yards,
but he heard God in Lake Michigan, which
was dark and moved in slippery metaphors.
Except dead men, though, nothing that grew in it
held any time that he could recognize,
so he came back.

Later the new barn burned in sullen sacrifice.
The wind was that unholy ill one; it threw
rattling clouds of hunger at the corn.
His wife paused in the day's work for a labor more
definitive, and died. He changed the baby while
the old farmers grinned but
hung around to help rebuild.
It seemed he must know something that the hogs did not.

He could find wind with a wetted finger,
but years went too fast to feel now.
Ploughing, he dreamed—the world was simplified,
and all that was Mind and what was not

were folded into one, and that was field.
What grew there, then, would be
essence, salvation, a crop to store
against eternal winters.
If it were men or some auspicious blend of corn
and men or love, he was absolved.
If something else, the hogs

were martyrs who had squealed the truth and gone to Heaven.
He meant to look. . . .

The cat, a skinny intuition, yowled against his leg.
He got up, dusted off his conscience,
headed for the barn.
Sun on the step went back, less brilliantly, to being sun.

PARATROOPER

From the dark side, feet first, breech birth, the fighter falls
and O the babe is small among perihelions
and his first breath crawls like a worm through impersonal
    countries
of no sins, but so many instinctive and unsatisfying suns.

And he falls like a scream from the nipple stars that stipple his
    passage
while with hands of wind and fear his body is bathed to the bone.
He tumbles and turns and yearns for a sign from the presences
who hurry in orbits beside him, unsmiling, adult, and not known.

What world is his, O orphan he is, in voids and valences
with cries that leave no answer in an enormous room—
Whose loss is his, no brother's or lover's, as wild he runs
through shadowed streets, and knocks at doors where no one is
    at home—

So fast and fierce he falls, and in vain he calls to the mother
for peace from the speed of his passage, the fire of his falling that
    blinds him
but his will flies out like an angered bird to peck at the foe
and memory, strongest myth, like a strange moth, opens behind
    him.

And now his course is slowed, his shoulders heavy now.
With the pull of angels-up and devils-down he is weak.
He feels the shame when the flu came when he was a little boy
and asafœtida, like an albatross, hung on his neck.

And now idea, pure unicorn in the air, he is riding
and the skies are hung, stars down, with crystalline streets of
    word
and zero, the dæmon that tormented him in school, is calling
but on his hand drops down the ripe, real dung of a bird.

And what of love, lost leaf, will he be finding now
like stray dogs that stopped to lick his hand and then ran on,
and what of hate, white heat, will he be feeling now
like the time the strange man kissed his mother when his father
    was out of town?

And is luck, bright rock on a string, strung safely around his neck
    now?
for he broke the wishbone at the home of his friend and got his
    hard-ball.
And is loss, black bird with the blooded beak, perched on his
    shoulder?
for the penny rolled away from his fingers and fell in a dark well.

But, see, the clouds roll back, some heavy homeland is shining.
In ascension, slow and silent, he goes to it in peace
and all the while white shadow, alter ego, follows after him
and he breaks through the membrane of history and sees the trees.

The thunder rises like mist and the leaves like lovers enfold him
and time, rocks, rooks and roses grow from his body, O blossomer,
    he.
And now he bends his knees and the delicate bones of his feet
strike earth, his short-haired, hell and heaven hard, maturity.

TO MY GODSON, ON HIS CHRISTENING

I

We've belled you, baby. Because the countryside here
is chasmed with alternatives, everyone likes to trace
each traveller; neighbors hear the noise of each choice.
Out in the open, now you'll ring your place.

Soon, out of these pricks and panics, rages,
hungerings, will mist into shape the toddling soul,
and we're pledged here to grab a dangle at the stairwell,
or kiss the skinned-up knees of a minor fall.

So you are a stranger who makes us meet, and estranger
too, for already our friends must look for each other
behind their parenthood, and learn on the familiar face
the unfamiliar features of mother and father.

Font, ceremony and babe have such classic contours,
that we, lifting you to your name, knowing
suddenly how smeared we are with trammeling, wish for
better posture, wisdom, a comelier showing.

Still, it's the human condition. Join us with charity,
whose deeds, like the little poet's metaphors
are good only in brave approximations,
who design, in walled-up workrooms, beautiful doors.

11

A lexicon, contrived for the time
he begins his serious games,
is our gift to the wordless child whose world
will hide till he calls its names.

Belong: to swim by controlling displacement; to please
your wavery element; the sea turtle's heavy ease.
Goodbye, goodbye: that dongs in the heart; that hits
where it's barest; said when the current of nearness quits.
Home: the place we make ourselves at. *How:*
a hook; it fishes; grapples; makes edgings toward know.
I love you, spoken or heard; burns schools, unskins
the toughest hider; wagers by guess, and wins.
Imagine: a thumb on the scales; saves beefs; gives praise
at a brief dinner. *Intelligence:* prisoner's base.
To give: dilates the I; is a brave bombarder
of hating; is hard. *Forgive:* synonym; harder.
Wishes: the bones we break in the days of chums
and secrets; amended later, make patienter limbs.
Words: a syllabled remnant of brotherhood.
Youth: a green apple; secretly, bitterly good.

III

Oh, we know our tongue tollings, baskets of wellwishes, won't
keep you back from your life. Still burnt from birth, you jump
toward that fire. Yet the pause we've programmed here is mis-
    leading,
whips me (balky, strange to the course and the speeding)
off, in a halter of words, to run for your meaning.

I've thought that the dream of the world is to bring, and again
    bring
out of a chaos of same, the irreplaceable thing,
so, when it dies, we may clap for that brilliant wasting.

To ground, water and air, from the showy heart of nature,
come such prodigal brimmings and breakings of creature
we can scarcely follow their sense. But they tie us to texture.

This black bubble eye of a pike, ringed with gold,
that neck-wattle, leaf veining, shell crimp, tailfeather, holds
marvel enough. But it's we who're the perfect, pure manifold.

Each sculp of feature is sole. Each skull encloses
trinkets, museums of rarities, whole zoos of wishes.
No one's repeated. We're spent; earth is dazzled with losses.

Farewell and farewell and farewell; yet we honor each going
with a feast of awareness whose richest flavor is knowing
our breed as snowflake; ourselves as yesterday's snowing.

And there's always something new under the sun

that warms toward our thaw. Look, the gifted air swarms
with it, falls from the weight of it, all those shapes, storms
of fresh possibilities. Now, spindling down, we see one
who'll drift near us. With special pleasure we watch you come.

NEW LAND

Consider now, stranger, how the new land lies
that broke through water before your eyes like a ping-pong ball
that the baby drowns in his bath. Precision instruments of body,
    brain
charted the way and the heart beat in the hold. It was no trick at
    all.

And you cannot claim the same fierce fear and pleasure
as when your friend pitched hay and scratched to view
the needle like a proverb's insight shining; or the time you saw
    the bottled message
bobbing on the sea and fished it out and found it was addressed to
    you.

Here on the unpublished land you have achieved
you plan to settle and you brought someone along
to sow in a neat garden the cabbages of your security. She in a
    starched housedress
and you in a snug belt will look at the sea for a long while from
    this home.

And yet you remember how short was the trip here in the trim
    vessel,
how the old albatross squawked in fear and flapped away
from the speeding steel, the sea snakes felt the shock in their
    scabby skins,
and only a fat gull hung to watch your passage under him, indif-
    ferent and gray.

The old man who sat on the pier and watched you start was al-
    ways talking
about Columbus whose heart turned old on the waters, thinking
    it right
to sail the other way, and never knew the island that he entered;
and how the rich bubbles of blood broke when Beowulf went
    under the water for his fight.

And about that one old sailor who murdered and mated,
bargained with gods to get the goal,
sometimes smote the sea with the bare oars of his arms, and after
twenty years
reached Ithaca, the certain country; but Socrates not in his life at
all.

O stranger, consider now the new land lying.
The trip was swift; the seas are free of bulldog boats now, blown
off the course, their crews' tongues blackening, their wracked
boards rank
with slime, while all the while their ignorant compasses point
home.

But though in your evening walk you stand on the sand and look
out,
fed by the garden and a girl's love like anemones, what will you
see,
who never knew, biting in the bones of the ship, the deep green
danger
that lifts and holds this island up to the retina, the reality?

DEATH BY ÆSTHETICS

Here is the doctor, an abstracted lover,
dressed as a virgin, coming to keep the tryst.
The patient was early; she is lovely; but yet
she is sick, his instruments will agree on this.

Is this the place, she wonders, and is he the one?
Yes, love is the healer, he will strip her bare,
and all his machinery of definition
tells her experience is costly here,

so she is reassured. The doctor approaches
and bends to her heart. But she sees him sprout like a tree
with metallic twigs on his fingers and blooms of chrome
at his eye and ear for the sterile ceremony.

Oh tight and tighter his rubber squeeze of her arm.
"Ahhh" she sighs at a chilly touch on her tongue.
Up the tubes her breath comes crying, as over her,
back and breast, he moves his silver thumb.

His fluoroscope hugs her. Soft the intemperate girl,
disordered. Willing she lies while he unfolds
her disease, but a stem of glass protects his fingertips
from her heat, nor will he catch her cold.

He peels her. Under the swaddling epiderm
her body is the same blue bush. Beautiful canals
course like a postcard scene that's sent him often.
He counts the *tiptup, tiptup* of her dutiful valves.

Pain hides like a sinner in her mesh of nerves.
But her symptoms constellate! Quickly he warms
to his consummation, while her fever flares
in its wick of vein, her wicked blood burns.

He hands her a paper. "Goodbye. Live quietly,
make some new friends. I've seen these stubborn cases
cured with time. My bill will arrive. Dear lady,
it's been a most enjoyable diagnosis."

She clings, but her fingers slip on his starchy dress.
"Don't leave me! Learn me! If this is all, you've swindled
my whole booty of meaning, where is my dearness?
Pore against pore, the delicate hairs commingled,

with cells and ligaments, tissue lapped on bone,
meet me, feel the way my body feels,
and in my bounty of dews, fluxes and seasons,
orifices, in my wastes and smells

see self. Self in the secret stones I chafed
to shape in my bladder. Out of a dream I fished
the ache that feeds in my stomach's weedy slough.
This tender swelling's the bud of my frosted wish.

Search out my mind's embroidery of scars.
My ichor runs to death so speedily,
spit up your text and taste my living texture.
Sweat to hunt me with love, and burn with me."

But he is gone. "Don't touch me," was all he answered.
"Separateness," says the paper. The world, we beg,
will keep her though she's caught its throbbing senses,
its bugs still swim in her breath, she's bright with its plague.

A RELATIVE AND AN ABSOLUTE

*It has been cool so far for December, but of course
the cold doesn't last long down here. The Bible is
being fulfilled so rapidly that it looks like it won't be
long until Jesus will come in the air, with a shout,
and all those who have accepted Jesus as their own
personal Saviour will be caught up to meet him and
then that terrible war will be on earth. The battle of
Armageddon. And all the unsaved people will have
to go through the great tribulation. Hope you are
both well. Bye.*

An aunt, my down-to-earth father's sibling, went to stay
in Texas, and had to continue by mail, still thanklessly,
her spiritual supervision of the family.

Texas orchards are fruitful. A card that would portray
this fact in green and orange, and even more colorfully say
on its back that Doom is nearly upon us, came regularly

at birthday, Easter and Christmas—and sometimes between the
    three.
That the days passed, and the years, never bothered her prophecy;
she restressed, renewed and remailed its imminence faithfully.

Most preaching was wrong, she felt, but found for her kin on
    Sunday,
in one voice on one radio station, one truth for all to obey.
Salvation being thus limited, it seemed to me

there was something unpleasant about that calm tenacity
of belief that so many others would suffer catastrophe
at any moment. She seemed too smug a protégée.

Otherwise, I rather liked her. Exchanging a recipe
or comparing winters with neighbors, she took life quietly
in a stuffy bungalow, among doilies of tatting and crochet.

A Relative and an Absolute

She had married late, and enjoyed the chance to baby
a husband, to simmer the wholesome vegetables and see
that vitamins squeezed from his fruit were drunk without delay.

Though she warned of cities and churches and germs, some
    modesty
or decorum, when face to face with us, wouldn't let her convey
her vision of Armageddon. But the post cards set it free.

It was hovering over the orange groves, she need only lay
her sewing aside, and the grandeur and rhythm of its poetry
came down and poured in her ear, her pencil moved eloquently.

She wrote it and wrote it. She will be "caught up," set free from
    her clay
as Christ comes "with a shout in the air" and trumpeting angels
    play,
and "the terrible war will be on earth" on that Judgment Day,

expecting all those years her extinction of body would be
attended by every creature, wrapped round in the tragedy
of the world, in its pandemonium and ecstasy.

When she died last winter, several relatives wrote to say
a kidney stone "as big as a peach pit" took her away.
Reading the letters, I thought, first of all, of the irony,

then, that I myself, though prepared to a certain degree,
will undoubtedly feel, when I lie there, as lonesome in death as she
and just as surprised at its trivial, domestic imagery.

A KIND OF MUSIC

*When consciousness begins to add diversity to its
intensity, its value is no longer absolute and inexpressible. The felt variations in its tone are attached
to the observed movement of its objects; in these objects its values are embedded. A world loaded with
dramatic values may thus arise in imagination; terrible and delightful presences may chase one another
across the void; life will be a kind of music made by
all the senses together. Many animals probably have
this kind of experience.* SANTAYANA

Irrelevance characterizes the behavior of our puppy.
In the middle of the night he decides that he wants to play,
runs off when he's called, when petted is liable to pee,
cowers at a twig and barks at his shadow or a tree,
grins at intruders and bites us in the leg suddenly.

No justification we humans have been able to see
applies to his actions. While we go by the time of day,
or the rules, or the notion of purpose or consistency,
he follows from moment to moment a sensuous medley
that keeps him both totally subject and totally free.

I'll have to admit, though, we've never been tempted to say
that he jumps up to greet us or puts his head on our knee
or licks us or lies at our feet irrelevantly.
When it comes to loving, we find ourselves forced to agree
all responses are reasons and no reason is necessary.

TOWARD A DEFINITION OF MARRIAGE

I

It is to make a fill, not find a land.
Elsewhere, often, one sights americas of awareness,
suddenly there they are, natural and anarchic,
with plantings scattered but rich, powers to be harnessed—
but this is more like building a World's Fair island.
Somebody thought it could be done, contracts are signed,
and now all materials are useful, everything; sludge
is scooped up and mixed with tin cans and fruit rinds,
even tomato pulp and lettuce leaves are solid
under pressure. Presently the ground humps up and shows.
But this marvel of engineering is not all.
A hodgepodge of creatures (no bestiary would suppose
such an improbable society) are at this time
turned loose to run on it, first shyly, then more free,
and must keep, for self's sake, wiles, anger, much of their
spiney or warted nature, yet learn courtesy.

II

It is closest to picaresque, but essentially artless.
If there were any experts, they are dead, it takes too long.
How could its structure be more than improvising,
when it never ends, but line after line plods on,
and none of the ho hum passages can be skipped?
It has a bulky knowledge, but what symbol comes anywhere near
suggesting it? No, the notion of art won't fit it—
unless—when it's embodied. For digression there
is meaningful, and takes such joy in the slopes and crannies
that every bony gesture is generous, full,
all lacy with veins and nerves. There, the spirit
smiles in its skin, and impassions and sweetens to style.
So this comes to resemble a poem found in his notebooks
after the master died. A charred, balky man, yet one day
as he worked at one of those monuments, the sun guiled him,

and he turned to a fresh page and simply let play
his great gift on a small ground. Yellowed, unpublished,
he might have forgotten he wrote it. (All this is surmise.)
But it's known by heart now; it rounded the steeliest shape
to shapeliness, it was so loving an exercise.

I I I

Or, think of it as a duel of amateurs.
These two have almost forgot how it started—in an alley,
impromptu, and with a real affront. One thought,
"He is not me," and one, "She is not me,"
and they were coming toward each other with sharp knives
when someone saw it was illegal, dragged them away,
bundled them into some curious canvas clothing,
and brought them to this gym that is almost dark, and empty.
Now, too close together for the length of the foils,
wet with fear, they dodge, stumble, strike,
and if either finally thinks he would rather be touched
than touch, he still must listen to the clang and tick
of his own compulsive parrying. Endless. Nothing
but a scream for help can make the authorities come.
If it ever turns into more of a dance than a duel,
it is only because, feeling more skillful, one
or the other steps back with some notion of grace
and looks at his partner. Then he is able to find
not a wire mask for his target, but a red heart
sewn on the breast like a simple valentine.

I V

If there's a Barnum way to show it, then think back
to a climax in the main tent. At the foot of the bleachers, a road
encloses the ringed acts; consider that as its design,
and consider whoever undertakes it as the whole parade
which, either as preview or summary, assures the public
hanging in hopeful suspense between balloons and peanutshells

that it's all worthwhile. The ponies never imagined
anything but this slow trot of ribbons and jinglebells.
An enormous usefulness constrains the leathery bulls
as they stomp on, and hardly ever run amuck.
The acrobats practised all their lives for this easy
contortion, and clowns are enacting a necessary joke
by harmless zigzags in and out of line.
But if the procession includes others less trustworthy?
When they first see the circle they think some ignorant
cartographer has blundered. The route is a lie,
drawn to be strict but full, drawn so each going forth
returns, returns to a more informed beginning.
And still a familiar movement might tempt them to try it,
but since what they know is not mentioned in the tromboning
of the march, neither the day-long pace of caged
impulse, nor the hurtle of night's terrible box-cars,
they shrink in their stripes and refuse; other performers
drive them out and around with whips and chairs.
They never tame, but may be taught to endure
the illusion of tameness. Year after year their paws
pad out the false curve, and their reluctant parading
extends the ritual's claim to its applause.

v

Say, for once, that the start is a pure vision
like the blind man's (though he couldn't keep it, trees
soon bleached to familiar) when the bandage came off
and what a world could be first fell on his eyes.
Say it's when campaigns are closest to home
that farsighted lawmakers oftenest lose their way.
And repeat what everyone knows and nobody wants
to remember, that always, always expediency
must freckle the fairest wishes. Say, when documents,
stiff with history, go right into the council chambers
and are rolled up to shake under noses, are constantly read from,
or pounded on, or passed around, the parchment limbers;

and, still later, if these old papers are still being shuffled,
commas will be missing, ashes will disfigure a word;
finally thumbprints will grease out whole phrases, the clear prose
won't mean much; it can never be wholly restored.
Curators mourn the perfect idea, for it crippled
outside of its case. Announce that at least it can move
in the imperfect action, beyond the windy oratory,
of marriage, which is the politics of love.

A TIME OF BEES
1964

ELEMENTARY ATTITUDES

I   EARTH

All spring the birds walked on this wormy world.
Now they avoid the ground, lining up on limbs
and fences, beaks held open, panting. And behold,
in a romper suit and tap shoes, my neighbor comes

click, click, past the gawking birds to her patio.
A middle-aged woman—they've known her for months, as have I,
coming down the side walk in a housedress twice a day
to throw them breadcrumbs and talk over the fence to me

as I weed and plant or write poems in the backyard garden.
Now I am dazzled by the flowers and by my neighbor in rompers.
She says it's hot, so hot, her house is like an oven.
Aren't the flowers bright, she says. They are worse

than bright these days, it seems to me, they are burning,
blazing in red salvia and orange daylilies,
in marigolds, in geraniums—even the petunias are turning
violent. Rose, red, orange, cerise,

yellow flame together and spread over their borders.
The earth and my diligent gardening, what have we done
to my neighbor? Arms wide out, she suddenly flutters
up into the air and comes down, and leaps again,

and clickety-clickety-clickety *rat-a-tat-tat*,
all over her patio she goes in a frenzy of tapdancing.
What new July conflagration is this, and what
would her husband say, who works in a drugstore? In the spring

she admired my jonquils and, later, the peonies calmly,
tossing bread to the birds as she chatted. They grew tamer and
     tamer.
Now they are squeaking and wheeling away from what they see,
and I am making good resolutions for next summer:

This collaboration with the earth should be done with care.
Even gardens, it seems, can set off explosions, and so
I'll have blue salvia and blue ageratum next year,
pale petunias, more poems, and some plumbago.

II   AIR

My primitive attitude toward the air makes it impossible
to be anything but provincial. I'll never climb Eiffels,
see Noh plays, big game, leprous beggars, implausible
rites, all in one lifetime. My friends think it's awful.

It leads to overcompensation: in the kitchen, prunes
in the potroast, kidneys in the wine and the restrained misery
of a hamburger-loving husband; in the yard, prone
plants from far places that never adjusted to Missouri;

in the mind, an unreasoning dislike of haiku, and in least
appropriate gatherings, innocent plans for the remission
of the world's woes—"Well, why don't we all just . . . ?"
People blush for me in political discussion.

It leads also, when visiting friends in California or reading
at the YMHA, to spending three-fourths of the time
on the way and only one-fourth of it there, and to travelling
always in the company of beginners. When I leave home

I ride with farm couples bringing the granddaughter back
for a visit, boys going off to their first big city,
honeymooners, college kids, toddlers who might get airsick,
and Texans who hire a whole car to get drunk cross-country.

Sooner or later most of these graduate to planes,
while I start out all over again on the ground.
The Texans and I are stuck with our beginnings.
To get a panoramic view of my own home town

I once took a helicopter ride and found everything unreal—
my house, lost in that vista half a mile under,

and whoever was grieving up there in a glass bubble,
pretending to enjoy the sights and growing blinder and blinder.

I can stand an outside view of myself, but nothing
about a bird's-eye view elevates or animates me in the slightest.
Maybe people who don't like air should just stop breathing.
I breathe, but I tend toward asthma and bronchitis.

III   FIRE

When feathers and fur came off, and the skin
bared, then we became open
to all manifestations of fire, to the sun's

inconceivable consummations. And I
was born in the busy-ness of that great day
of heat and light, hunting with my whole body.

The blood boils. "A higher temperature,
by hastening the chemical reactions of the creature,
allows it to live more quickly and more

intensely." Biologists are in favor of burning,
and I too, creature singeing
to certain death in the metabolic blessing,

I too celebrate my fires. In Maine
the treetops came sizzling down and I ran
with chipmunks and foxes. Utterances, mean

or stealthy or rhymed, charged, live,
fall all day on the tindery nerves.
These ignitions, and those in the stove

of my flesh, underhand, and speculations,
and barbecue and fireplace in their seasons
keep me quick. Cigarettes blazon

me to words, and bourbon. Some eyes
are best sparks. Our stuff multiplies
in warmth, we are lovers from the first ceremonies

of protein, the lonesome cold stars
miss us. A first breath, and our natures
are afire, we run in the blistering years.

IV   WATER

It is hard to remember what one is mostly made of.
Floating on top, as ark, is a sort of sieve
carrying my wet brain, and under the waves
ovaries and liver and other items sway
like the bulbs and stems of some aquatic lily.

But even here, at the confluence of the Missouri
and the Mississippi, late summers are dry
and there is little snow in winter. Abstractions are the key
to being. Scientists flourish, but swimmers
are bitten to death by catfish in these rivers.

When I landed, out of the broken bag of my mother,
heat and buoyancy had to be learned all over,
but there are few such dangerous floods, so far.
On humid days, under a green sea of oak leaves,
I move secretly, like a skin-diver, but don't dive.

The mind is seldom wholly immersed. We live
willingly, fear both drouth and drowning, conceive
in swampy places, and drink to provoke love.
When love's unkindness punctures the eyeball, tears
remind us again that we are made of water.

A SERIOUS CASE

"The [life of] the democratic man . . is motley and manifold and . . this distracted existence he terms . . freedom."
"The perfect guardian of our State must be a philosopher . . he whose mind is fixed on true being."
"It will be our duty to select . . natures which are fitted for the task of [protecting] our City . . quick to see and swift to overtake the enemy."
"Carpenters and smiths and many other artisans will be sharers in our little State . . and salesmen . . hunters . . servants . . tutors . . nurses . . barbers . . cooks."
"The artist . . knows nothing of true existence . . Let this be our defence for sending [him] away . . for the safety of the City."

If we happen to choke up on history, none too soon
we resort to "The Republic." A receptionist lets us in
at the door we're driven to, on acres of sedative green
or the city's edge. Let theory save us, if it can.

When all the white rats in the world have confirmed our flaws,
and the separateness of our wish, or its treaty with laws
where either night causes day or there is no cause
is cramped in a formula every bright youngster knows,

we'll see what we'll see. In the meantime, Plato will do
for rest in a dream some two thousand years ago.
White-coated experts have classified us, and now
the door whispers shut, whatever is here is true.

Top floor, Ward Three: Exalted thinkers roam
and bump harmlessly into abstractions outside their own
abstraction. With each, disguised out of deference to brain,
is his earthly form, sacked in a rough white gown

over rough white pajamas. Here every head has to make
an experiment that might startle even the smart Greek—
to design a New Order, yes, but then bring it the whole meek
self as citizen, and try out how it will work.

Habit, the human stance, inviolateness of symbol,
the universal fable of appearance—all fail
under such a ferocious demand that truth out and time tell.
A. paces off life's length from wall to wall.

B., in a quiet corner, concealed by her hair
thrown over her face, has bombed the earth for an hour,
but will glue it together again, this time in a square.
C. points at sinful God sneaking under a chair.

D. is led out and shut up. Alas, he found
neither justice nor mercy would function in his State of Mind,
and his torment's too loud. E., on his knees, is enthroned.
F. tightens his logic, and notes how the windowblind,

the cup of milk, a black playing card and a word
confirm his premises. (But, sorry for such absurd
and total commitment, observers are fighting it hard;
they stun these out after a while, and restock the ward.)

Middle floor, Ward Two: Brought away from his barracks, his
    aim,
his practice maneuvers, locked in a living room,
is the man of action whose dedication is grim
and steadfast—to find the foul enemy and destroy him.

Held together, all agree that delay is despair
although nothing has ever defined the foe but the mirror.
With pills and injections, bars at the window and door,
propagandists persuade them to wait, there is no war.

But they cling to their girding for battle—crumpled clothes,
loose shoelaces, straggly hair. As a calming ruse,
all calls to duty are silenced, yet often at agonized
attention they slump, with bent head and cast-down eyes.

The Ideal encloses them neatly. What else would condone
such transcendent ardor? Each follows orders within
himself. Each is the hero who will act alone.
Even when disarmed, with nailfiles, neckties, pins,

deodorants and belts removed, J. will pick at his face,
K., who is clever and devious, for weeks will refuse
or vomit his food, L. weeps at the pacifist disgrace
of her breathing, while M. tries cheer as a trick for release.

Quiet till now in his forced retreat, N. suddenly
cries "Help!" at the window. He's watched. Twice more, and
    they'll see
that he's turned philosopher, has to be sent to Ward Three.
(But this kind of misfortune could happen in any army.)

First floor, Ward One: The populace mills all over,
layers of the daily groundwork, tireless re-weavers
of meaning by repetition, tunnellers by clever
hands and wits in the trivia of human endeavor.

But seldom outside do we see such dramatically pure
representatives. Each is an all too genuine character,
and one domestic virtue or vice is made clear
through the action of each, as in children's literature.

Q. is HELPFUL—all day will chat, will roll
R.'s hair into pincurls, wind up a skein of wool
for S., sew a button on T.; (but in the dark lull
of night lies hunting, can find no friends at all).

(Though she kept to her room at home,) SHY R. now and then
will accept U.'s (trembling) offer of a magazine—
he is NERVOUS. X., who is FEARFUL (of pigeons and men)
smiles at a crooner held back by the TV screen.

S., the CRITICAL, knits. But the yarn is too coarse
and too green, the room too warm. Yesterday was worse,
chilly, with spotted lettuce at lunch, squeaky doors.
(Her sensitive skin breaks out at all things, their perverse

imperfection.) No one's as HAPPY as T. The wreck
of a lifetime, in fact the whole ridiculous mistake
of being, makes him laugh out loud. (But employers will seek
a humor more business-like, a more practical joke.)

V.'s INDECISIVE (and mornings for him are hell—
which sock should he put on first?) Afternoons he does well,
plays pingpong with W. (who tests his own motives until
he faints in the evenings), being CONSCIENTIOUS. The smell

of X.'s perfume, her heeltaps, her satin swish
announce she is VAIN. (Three husbands have left her, she's
      rushed
to death, screams Stop! Stop! at the dizzying push
of wrinkles in loneliness.) Y.'s perpetual blush

only means that she's ANXIOUS. (Her face is hot but sweat
trickles cold on her leg, for the worst hasn't happened yet.)
Z.—but this ward is jammed. Even sampling it
takes far too long, and we've run out of alphabet.

Well, our scholarly sojourn is over. We must go.
We'll pay, of course, for the privilege of saying goodbye
to past ideas. Electricity, chemistry, industry,
understanding, love and time all took us away

from the classic Statesman. A hard democracy
reinstates us. It yields to the flow of Becoming freely
and moves with that aimless mixture of water and debris,
but its manner of movement aims at the possibility

that home-made restrictions may heal the lunatic will
and that heart and mind, though classless, may be schooled well
by each other. Boatless and untherapeutic, its control
neither supports nor simplifies the individual,

who becomes, in a fluid condition of rule and river,
all wards in one, the dreamer, the doer and the lover
of life's detail. He becomes, in fact, a survivor
of the kind Plato banished, knowing he would scramble all over

and scuttle the Ark. To swim, mixing grace with reason,
interfering with form for the sake of personal motion
and working with constant depth in the currents of season
is his stately duty; to sink, his forgiveable treason.

RECOVERY

I   THE DORMITORY

In Mexico the little mixed herds come home in the evening,
slow through that hard-colored landscape, all driven together—
the hens, a few pigs, a burro, two cows, and the thin
perro that is everywhere. It is the same scene here.

The nurses herd us. In our snouts and feathers
we move through the rigid cactus shapes of chairs
colored to lie, belie terror and worse.
Assorted and unlikely as the lives we bear,

we go together to bed, one dozen of us.
It was a hard day's grazing, we fed on spines of courtesy
and scratched up a few dry bugs of kindness.
But we deserved less than that generosity.

Our teats of giving hang dry. Our poor peons are bewildered
and poorer still, the whole landscape is impoverished
by the unnatural economy of this group's greed,
whose bark is bitter, who are swaybacked, fruitless, unfleshed.

The pen echoes to a meaningless moo, "I want to go home,"
one cackles over sins, one yaps in rhythmic complaining,
but those shapes under the sheets are not like mine.
We are locked in unlove. I am sick of my own braying.

The metaphor shakes like my hand. Come, Prince of Pills,
electric kiss, undo us, and we will appear
wearing each other's pain like silk, the awful
richness of feeling we blame, but barely remember.

II   THE DOCTORS

Those who come from outside are truly foreign.
How are we to believe in the clear-eyed and clean-shaven?

Recovery

The jungle I crawl through on my hands and knees,
the whole monstrous ferny land of my own nerves,
hisses and quakes at these upright missionaries
wearing immaculate coats, and will not open.

Mine is waiting outside like a mild boy.
He is unarmed, he will never make it to this anarchy.
Somewhere down his civil streams, through his system,
a survivor came babbling, half-wild from stink and sun,
and news leaked out about our savage customs.
I bit my bloody heart again today.

At night I dream of tables and chairs, beds,
hospitals. I wake. I am up to my waist in mud.
Everything shrieks, cloudbursts of confusion are beating
on my head as I twist and grab for vines, sweating
to make a raft, to tie something together. He is waiting.
I want his words after all, those cheap beads.

Stranger, forgive me, I have clawed as close as I can.
Your trinkets clink to the ground, it is all dark
on the other side of my impenetrable network.
I will wallow and gnaw—but wait, you are coming back,
and at touch, flamethrower, underbrush goes down.
Now I can stand by you, fellow-citizen.

III   A MEMORY

"Write a letter to Grandpa," my mother said, but he smelled old.
"He'll give you something nice," she said, but I was afraid.
He never looked at me, he muttered to himself, and he hid
bad things to drink all over his house, and Grandma cried.
A gray stranger with a yellowed mustache, why should I have
    mailed
my very first message to him? Well, consider the innocent need
that harries us all: "Your Aunt Callie thinks she's smart, but *her*
    kid
never sent her first letter to Pa." (To hold her I had to be good.)
"You've learned to write. Write Grandpa!" she said, so I did.

It was hard work. "Dear Grandpa, How are you, I am fine,"
but I couldn't come to the end of a word when I came to the
margin,
and the lines weren't straight on the page. I erased that paper so
thin
you could almost see through it in spots. I couldn't seem to learn
to look ahead. (Mother, remember we both had to win.)
"We are coming to visit you next Sunday if it does not rain.
Yours truly, your loving granddaughter, Mona Van Duyn."
That Sunday he took me aside and gave me the biggest coin
I ever had, and I ran away from the old man.

"Look, Mother, what Grandpa gave me. And as soon as I get back
home
I'll write him again for another half dollar." But Mother said
"Shame!"
and so I was ashamed. But I think at that stage of the game,
or any stage of the game, things are almost what they seem
and the exchange was fair. Later in the afternoon I caught him.
"Medicine," he said, but he must have known his chances were
slim.
People don't hide behind the big fern, I wasn't dumb,
and I was Grandma's girl. "So, *Liebling*, don't tell them,"
he said, but that sneaky smile called me by my real name.

Complicity I understood. What human twig isn't bent
by the hidden weight of its wish for some strict covenant?
"Are you going to tell?" he wanted to know, and I said, "No, I
won't."
He looked right at me and straightened his mouth and said, "So,
Kind,
we fool them yet," and it seemed to me I knew what he meant.
Then he reached in his pocket and pulled out two candies covered
with lint,
and we stood there and each sucked one. "*Ja*, us two, we know
what we want."
When he leaned down to chuck my chin I caught my first
Grandpa-scent.
Oh, it was a sweet seduction on pillows of peppermint!

Recovery

And now, in the middle of life, I'd like to learn how to forgive
the heart's grandpa, mother and kid, the hard ways we have to
    love.

IV   BY THE POND IN THE PARK, BY THE
HOSPITAL

The grass is green, the trees and the bench are green.
Parked cars, like aquarium pebbles, circle the pond.
A roar, a dry sprinkle, and a good machine
goes by, cutting grass in a ten-foot strip. In the wind
walk blackbirds. This is the closest I've ever been
to an elegant, high-stepping one. He is watching my hand
and I, watching his red and yellow wing, am sane.

Little dandy, your chemistry, and not your fine
feather, dazzles my half-familiar head,
for, three blocks back, marvelous returns are routine
and the simple map to decay unreadable, or unread.
—To trust perception again is like learning to lean
on water. The water, moving over minnows, is haunted.
Dandelions bloom, the trees and the grass are green.

In the hospital, other matters go on, the obscene
writhing of feelings like worms on hooks, and all mute,
all smelling of wild loss; and now the mowing man
stops and dismounts, throws something in the pond, something
    light,
then starts up his motors—an empty coffee tin
that scares the minnows away, sinking in the rot
of leaves, to the bottom. That inundation was a dream.

All around the pond a bracelet of cars is curled
and the wind smells green through the mower's unerring noise.
I think through my senses, I chew grass, and a squirrel
chews too, but something hard. Melodrama never has
real answers. Memory will come, like some quiet girl,
slow-spoken and friendly, to tell me whatever it was
I knew I wanted in this grassy world.

AN ESSAY ON CRITICISM

Standing in the kitchen, ready to rip open the tinfoil,
I paused to appreciate how abstraction flatters my will,

how efficiently it takes out of time the qualities I can use
and rejects the others. Assuming onion soup as my purpose,

the onions in my cupboard, which used to be, so to speak, real,
insisted on their whole nature, were never so sweetly under
    control—

they were always inconveniently rotting or trying to bloom
or spraying my eyes with perverse misdirection of their perfume,

while these neat and peaceful little particles will go into the steam,
inoffensive to my notions of what an onion or a tear humanly
    means,

and come simmering back to what might be called onions again,
or stay on the shelf, drily possible, inert until I need them.

I had paused with the package, as I say, but at the doorbell's ring
I went and let in a friend whose radiance was transforming.

"Let me tell you this minute!" she cried, and just inside the door
clutched at my sleeve and held me to her eloquence like the
    Mariner.

"His name doesn't matter—he won't know—for my future he is
    no one—
but I know now—I've learned what love is—how love is like a
    poem—

how it 'makes nothing happen,' how it 'lies in the valley of its
    saying,'
how it lives by its tensions with the roundness and perfection of
    a daydream,

how it delights in itself, doubles back on itself, is 'to be'
in the full awareness of its being, its own elegance of play,

is an equilibrium of sound, sight and sense all together
springing to vehement life and celebrating each other,

how it finds what it wants from reality and makes up the rest,
but is finally its own reference, exists in its own interest,

how it kindles the world that is made, the lie that has made it,
the mind's grasp, the heart's hold, the senses' rich hauls of the
    scoop-net,

and while passion, which is only its paraphrase, dies of quick
    pleasure,
it survives in its difficult wholeness, its ceremonious self-enclosure,

beyond sincerity, an exclusive configuration
that includes me in art, lets me say, 'This is *my* creation!'

Oh, I'm only an amateur," she said, a young woman and poet,
"but you know all about it," to me, enough older to deny it,

and she stopped and waited, and I stood like a rebellious nun
whose habit is read too simply in the sense of separation.

Beginners have ignorance as their danger and precious privilege,
but re-beginners suffer and fail through distrust of knowledge.

Yet I looked, out of vanity, for an honest advisory role
and turned up a lack of innocence, at least, that might be helpful;

for, once one has trembled through an eavesdrop on private con-
    fession,
one writes to Dear Someone Somewhere, assuming mutual in-
    discretion.

"You're published now," I told her, "in your eyes, your whole
   air,
so your poem is half of the truth, the other half is the reader.

All you've described, that enchanted, self-created 'self-enclosure,'
is made to lie in print in an enchanting self-exposure

to the one who, having by accident or inquisitiveness
turned to its page, puts all his perception at its service,

by understanding goes on past its artful shyness
to its artful appeal, and through that to its real fineness,

'suspends disbelief' that its loving selection is total,
forgets what it doesn't mention, the dust on the windowsill,

the office routine, any routine, and . . . beholds.
Later, of course, come tests more critically controlled,

but a poem, believe me, by consent, never by coercion,
slowly, deeply, seriously can move another person,

for, although the instant of judgment it starts from is spontaneous,
unwilled, the rest of its painful and painstaking fuss

results from the pressure of a passionately serious wish
on invention which would rather be carefree, playful, coltish—

the 'wish to be believed.' A poem exerts an intention
of passing all tests, of standing as permanent intervention

between reader and reader-as-he-was. I just mean," I ended,
"being written and published, something is somehow being said."

She thanked me, looking somewhat thoughtful, and said goodbye,
   and left,

and I gripped in turn, from long practice, a theoretical Wedding
    Guest,

confessing to someone less starry-eyed than she about engage-
    ments
how the belief that to be believed is always of consequence

comes to hang on the pencil, heavy, and how merely growing old
makes all moving weightier and more expensive—time favors the
    household—

yet a poem's way of happening won't let anything happen at all
unless it is serious—it is no brothel and has no windfalls;

and how, though it's not for its own sake, pure revel in its own
    nature,
it must keep its salutation secret and be written as if it were,

expressing the contradiction that only this professional lie
permits the collaboration that can make it come true;

and how a reader who comes to take in the surprise of each path-
    way
in a world of formal difference and difference of personality

may find other surprises. (There is one, impressed as trailbreaker,
who returns to the poem as a kind of conscientious marriage-
    broker

and raps it and taps it and maps it clear back to a region
where the writer stands shivering in the art as artless human

and takes down her measurements—but we needn't worry about
    him;
he bundled up for the chill, reached that climate as professional
    pilgrim.)

But there's one who goes back to his business so provoked by the
    tour
he denounces the vacation, swears he won't take it any more,

but on the way to the office finds he is walking to its rhythm
and changes his stride, but its rhyme goes bing-bong in his bosom,

tries TV at night, but its imagery covers his screen,
and closes his eyes but his memory insists on its meaning,

and finds that it is modifying the dust on his windowsill
and its sum is including parts much greater than its whole,

until, willing to do something, he makes an apprehensive return
and runs through the foreign scenery, feeling strangely at home

(for what other world is there but the one we believe to be,
that we touch and are touched by in affections, conceptions and
    body?),

till he reaches an ultimate region and sees, standing there,
himself and the writer, two humans, artless and similar—

a likeness proved out of difference—and, enlightened in its
    sunshine,
he sees they've been caring about each other the whole time,

and so, through its other active agent, the poem is a power,
and the responsibility . . .

                but it was almost time for dinner.

All of a sudden, when I went back into the kitchen,
tears came to my eyes, galvanized by a sort of pain.

Now of course I remember perfectly all that was going on
at the start, but it wasn't leading to empathy with the onion.

The inner life of that bulb would never come to interest me;
I am not like an onion, I don't wish anyone else to be.

I was only using the onion. It is only useful,
and, defining it by so few qualities, I make it immortal

and agree with the science of onions that all onions are the same
and don't see what is individual. I don't have time.

Was the pang for poetry? I meant to take time for that,
for what is gentle, idealistic and fair and, in the long run, right.

I wasn't just using poetry. I was caring about it.
I believe life wouldn't be nearly so meaningful without it.

I want them illuminating each other as much as possible,
and in the foregoing, whenever their likeness grew implausible,

whenever the see-saw poise of the metaphor weakened,
I held up the poem's side first, and life's side second,

for I believe in art's process of working through otherness to
    recognition
and in its power that comes from acceptance, and not imposition—

for people, that is; and if life is not a poem, and this is clear,
one can still imply that one sometimes wishes it were.

As I emptied out the tinfoil package, tears fell in the pot
as if onionjuice had caused them; the important thing is, it had not.

Let technology salt the soup, let it remove every eye-sting
that has no necessitous human predicament as its meaning.

These tears can season only if they fall on a shoulder
and a breathing, feeling recipient responds to their moisture,

but poetry didn't cause them either. The pain, that tearjerk,
was life, asserting its primacy in a well-timed rebuke,

and the assertion is valid. A poem can stay formally seated
till its person-to-person call, centuries later, is completed,

being abstract enough to afford inertness on the shelf
and yet being the self's own lifelike abstraction of itself.

But these tears, I remind, well and fall in a room with a clock.
Out of action they come, into action they intend to hurry back.

Their message is more vital than their grace can be, and when they
    speak
they adopt with justice the imperfect urgency of rhetoric,

basing their case on unearned, inglorious similarity:
"Dear reader, there is nothing immortal about the you and the me.

We must move in time, time moves, we must care right away!"
Less beautifully patient than a poem, one might call them an essay.

POT-AU-FEU

Everything that is going on in Nature . . . in-crease[s] the entropy of the part of the world where it is going on. A living organism . . . tends to approach the state of maximum entropy, which is death. It is continually sucking orderliness from its environment [and] freeing itself from all the entropy it cannot help producing . . . [and] thus it evades the decay to thermodynamical equilibrium.

SCHRÖDINGER, What is Life?

I remembered how Mrs. Procter once said to me that, having had a long life of many troubles, sufferings, encumbrances and devastations, it was, in the evening of that life, a singular pleasure, a deeply felt luxury, to her, to sit and read a book: the mere sense of the security of it, the sense that, with all she had outlived, nothing could now happen, was so great within her.

HENRY JAMES, Notebooks

It is all too clear that order wasn't our invention.
What we thought we imposed on Nature was her own intention,
and if anyone doubts it, let's see who's the steady old hand
at doting arrangement, her metabolism or our mind:
Watch her anticipate our cellular howl
by spooning out stable linkings of chemical gruel,
or, using the disorder that is death to us,
producing more anchovies and asparagus,
or, for our snacks, slicing up without pause or limit
a million billion other lives a minute.

But, lo, in the high society of consciousness,
we diet to death on our own affectional fuss,
rocking the environment through disordering lips
with the erratic heat motion of our relationships,
turning living to losing, burning with need for our fellow
and filling the air with exhaust for him to swallow;
for to feed on trouble and void a composed overhaul
takes a structure humbler than man's, and more Natural.

Yet since mind and body are under each other's thumb
and you come to my mind, something really ought to be done.

You'll have to admit, my darling, that we tire each other,
exhaling such smogs of entropy that the weather
is unwholesome here for us in our weakened condition.
Already we're worn from testing an important mutation
of the internal scene, and we've used lots of heat to start
taking off on those dizzying quantum jumps of the heart,
yet we're forced to keep on regenerating the nicks
of a thousand daily empathic enzyme kicks,
and to carry, wherever we go in our hungry waning,
the sweet encumbrance of one another's meaning.

And so, to balance the emotional wear-and-tear,
let me set a table in the atmosphere.
They say if a glassful of marked molecules were poured
in the Seven Seas, and diligently stirred,
then in any glassful dipped from any ocean
you'd find one hundred out of the original potion.
I can't prove a poem's caloric count is so high,
nor know my particular measuring will reach your eye,
but I'll pour by faith, and believe that wherever you sup
the nourishing orderliness has been thickened up.

The move is mine, my sex is less prone to the torment
of organic dignity, and more attached to our ferment.
I'll debase my system, I'll eat like a weed, and exchange
sounds that I've simmered down to predictable range,
a feast of patterning, a treat of tended lines,
and visible forms, toothsome as tenderloins,
to keep you, sucking the images that bring
you close to receive this artful cherishing,
an inexhaustible fountain of passionate waste
while I grow and blossom on its deathy taste.

59

POSTSCRIPT:

Watch out, Mrs. Procter, you'll be warmed against your will!
All that jiggling, perverse and thermodynamical,
may suddenly start up again, those turning pages
may tip you right out into life's economic outrages—
and you who have grown so gentle and groomed and tidy
there on the settee, a thoroughly astonished lady
of equilibristic luxury, with a paper plaything,
will burst into metabolic huckstering
and steam back, stoked up on innocent-seeming print,
into devastations, into love's dishevelment.

GRAY'S APOCRYPHA

On page 1003 of the anatomy text,
in a chapter not used by surgeons and therapists,
consider an illustration, in such pastels
as the heart rarely hears of, shaped like a loose fist,

of the heart. Tubes feed into it from the ear and eye
and fingertips—these are roughly sketched at the margins—
and, tumbling down the tubes, the elements are shown
on their way to the chamber. Some are somewhat like pigeons,

and will flutter and call when they get inside, some
are more like yoyos, running up and down from a fixed
point, but some like oranges roll and peel
and others slip to the bottom like syrup, relaxed.

The heart fills. Each day the heart fills.
In that resonant cave the clutter grows more and more rich,
the calls accumulate, motion reflects from the walls,
there is flight, fall, flurry—finally there is so much

felt that the main valve opens, the heart convulses,
and up a great duct to the mouth it all will pour,
to be mushed there and shaped into words, "dear," "my dear,"
the lips will open and out come "my love," and more.

In the rest of the book our innards came as a shock,
those vacant structures whose juicy dealings hurt
our sense of ourselves—but here it is mostly true.
You know it, I know it, this is what happens in the heart.

And now, on page 1004, consider the heart
in a morbid condition. Those sucking scouts have sent
from out of the air such food as they could find,
and filled the fist. But what awful discontent

the drawing describes! All tubes are clogged, swollen
with stuff, feathers and rotting peels pack
every inch above the sticky bottom,
which is roiled. All movement has batted itself sick

against the growing pressure. What has gone wrong?
See, at the top of the main duct leading out
the trouble's plain. Some outside atmosphere,
unbenign, has sealed the lips. In a great clutch

the heart heaves, and again, to rid itself
of its congestion, then hangs, bulged and sore,
sagging the chest. This will go on. Oh God,
you knew it, I knew it, there is no known cure.

NOTES FROM A SUBURBAN HEART

Freud says that ideas are libidinal cathexes, that is to say, acts of love.

NORMAN O. BROWN

It's time to put fertilizer on the grass again.
The last time I bought it, the stuff was smelly and black,
and said "made from Philadelphia sewage" on the sack.
It's true that the grass shot up in a violent green,
but my grass-roots patriotism tells me to stick
to St. Louis sewage, and if the Mississippi isn't thick
enough to put in a bag and spread on a lawn,
I'll sprinkle 5-10-5 from nobody's home,
that is to say . . .

it's been a long winter. The new feeder scared off the birds
for the first month it was up. Those stupid starvelings,
puffed up like popcorn against the cold, thought the thing
was a death-trap. The seeds and suet on its boards
go down their gullets now, and come out song,
but scot-free bugs slit up the garden. It is spring.
I've "made bums out of the birdies," in my next-door neighbor's
    words,
that is to say . . .

your life is as much a mystery to me as ever.
The dog pretends to bite fleas out of sheer boredom,
and not even the daffodils know if it's safe to come
up for air in this crazy, hot-and-cold weather.
Recognitions are shy, the faintest tint of skin
that says we are opening up, is it the same
as it was last year? Who can remember that either?
That is to say,

I love you, in my dim-witted way.

QUEBEC SUITE

for Robert Wykes, Composer

I

Every evening
in this old valley
a bird, a little brown bird
says thanks
like a sleepy hen
for red
berries.

II

The farmer sits in the sun
and sends nine kids out to work in all directions.
The baby sits on his lap, the toddler leans on his knee.
We have to buy some fishing worms, *les vers.*
"Vingt-cinq vers, s'il vous plait."
A tow-head boy runs for the can of worms. *"Fait chaud
     aujourdhui."*
How pleasant it is.
The sun shines on the thin farm.
The lazy farmer beams at his busy children.
We make the dog howl for the baby.
"Ecoute," the farmer tells his child,
"il parle.
Ecoute,
il parle."

III

The dog changes
here in the open, in wild country.
He wanders with chipmunks,
he saw a moose,

birds beset him,
the skunk under the cabin makes his hair go up.
He spreads his toes to walk the dock
over gaps in the boards
and looks at the lake with calculation.
He is another animal.

IV

I am afraid to swim in this water,
it is so thick with life.
One stranger after another
comes out of it. Right by the boat
there rose at dusk the otter,
dark and slick, as if covered with ointment.
I said, "My God, an alligator!"
And the pike comes up, his vacant golden eye
staring away from the hook.
Perhaps there are eels down under,
looking up at the skating bugs.
In Quebec there is no alligator,
but I see many a stranger.

V

The rocky beaches
are covered with blueberries.
I thought they were blue flowers at first.
Now we use them in pie and pancake,
but still they look like flowers.
Hazy blue,
their smoke rubs off with one touch of the finger.
Under that smear
a deeper blue appears,
as rich and dark as anything we earn.
And so this country feeds our hungers.

V I

The loon is yodeling.
My favorite waterfowl, sleek and swarthy,
a master duck,
he will swim under half the lake
before he comes up with his catch, flapping and swallowing.
But strong as he is, brave as he is,
he is a lonesome bird.
He and his mate must touch each other
all day long across the water
with their cries:
"Here. Here I am. And you? You?"
"Yes, I am here. And you? You? You? You? You?"

EARTH TREMORS FELT IN MISSOURI

The quake last night was nothing personal,
you told me this morning. I think one always wonders,
unless, of course, something is visible: tremors
that take us, private and willy-nilly, are usual.

But the earth said last night that what I feel,
you feel; what secretly moves you, moves me.
One small, sensuous catastrophe
makes inklings letters, spelled in a worldly tremble.

The earth, with others on it, turns in its course
as we turn toward each other, less than ourselves, gross,
mindless, more than we were. Pebbles, we swell
to planets, nearing the universal roll,
in our conceit even comprehending the sun,
whose bright ordeal leaves cool men woebegone.

A GARLAND FOR CHRISTOPHER SMART

I

"For the flower glorifies God and the root parries the adversary. For the right names of flowers are yet in heaven. God make gardners better Nomenclators."

For cosmos, which has too much to live up to,
for hyacinth, which stands for all the accidents of love,
for sunflower, whose leanings we can well understand, for
    foxglove
and buttercup and snapdragon and candytuft and rue,

and for baby'sbreath, whose pre-Freudian white we value,
and for daisy, whose little sun confronts the big one
without despair, we thank good gardeners who pun
with eye and heart, who wind the great corkscrew

of naming into the cork on what we know.
While the root parries the adversary, the rest
nuzzles upward through pressure to openness,
and grows toward its name and toward its brightness and sorrow.

And we pray to be better nomenclators, at home
and in field, for the sake of the eye and heart and the claim
of all who come up without their right names,
of all that comes up without its right name.

I I

"For I bless God for the Postmaster General and all conveyancers of letters under his care especially Allen and Shelvock."

Pastor of these paper multitudes,
the white flocks of our thought that run back and forth,
preserve the coming and going of each nickel's worth
that grazed on the slope of the brain or trotted from its inroads.

And all proxies who step to the door in the stead of the upper
left hand corner, keep coming to every house,
that even the most feeble narration may find its use
when it falls into the final slot of the eye, that the mapper

of human dimension may distend that globe each day
and draw each day the connecting network of lines
that greetings and soapflake coupons and valentines
make between one heart and another. We pray

especially for the postman with a built-up shoe who likes dogs
and the one at the parcel post window who bears with good grace
the stupid questions of ladies, and we especially bless
the back under every pack, and the hands, and the legs.

III

*"Let Huldah bless with the Silkworm—the ornaments of the Proud are
from the Bowells of their Betters."*

It was a proud doorway where we saw the spider drop
and swing to drop and swing his silk, the whole
spider rose to raise it, to lower it, fell,
and dangled to make that work out of his drip.

Not speculation, but art. Likewise the honeypot
that makes a fine table, an ornament to bread.
The bees danced out its plot, and feed our pride,
and milked themselves of it, and make us sweet.

And long library shelves make proud homes.
One line, a day in Bedlam, one book, a life
sometimes, sweated onto paper. What king is half
so high as he who owns ten thousand poems?

And the world is lifted up with even more humble words,
snail-scum and limey droppings and fly-blow

and gold loops that dogs have wetted on snow—
all coming and going of beasts and bugs and birds.

IV

"Let Jamen rejoice with the bittern blessed be the name of Jesus for
Denver Sluice, Ruston, and the draining of the fens."

And let any system of sewage that prospers say,
"I am guide and keeper of the human mess,
signature in offal of who, over the face
of the great globe, moves, and is the great globe's glory."

And any long paving, let it utter aloud,
"I bear the coming together and the going apart
of one whose spirit-and-dirt my spirit-and-dirt
eases in passage, for the earth cherishes his load."

Let drainage ditches praise themselves, let them shout,
"I serve his needs for damp and dryness." Let mansions
cry, "We extend his name with our extensions,"
and let prefabricated houses bruit

their mounting up in a moment to preserve this creature.
Let the great globe, which rolls in the only right air,
say, "He delves me and heaps me, he shapes without fear,
he has me in his care, let him take care."

V

"For he purrs in thankfulness when God tells him he's a good cat.
For the divine spirit comes about his body to sustain it in compleat cat.
For he camels his back to bear the first notion of business."

But let those who invest themselves in the dumb beast
go bankrupt gladly at the end of this investment,
for in answering dumb needs he is most eloquent,
but in sickness cannot ask help, and is often lost.

His smell reaches heaven, hope and faith are his fragrance.
Whether he camels his back or barks, he wears our harness,
he sits under our hearts through all his days, questionless.
His tail directs orchestras of joy at our presence.

For his nature he shivers his coat to cast off flies.
For his nature he hisses, or milks the cushion with his claws.
But he will follow our leg forever, he will give up his mouse,
he will lift up his witless face to answer our voice.

And when he burnishes our ankles or turns away from his breed
to sit beside ours, it may be that God reaches out of heaven
and pets him and tells him he's good, for love has been given.
We live a long time, and God knows it is love we need.

A SENTIMENTAL DELUSION

> *. . . There will perhaps be some men we will not love, and some machines to which we will become attached. If we find a being which looks and behaves like other men and is beyond our capacity ever to love, we must say of it that it is only a machine. . . . Should we find a machine which we can love, we must say of it that it has a human nature and human powers . . . I preserve my humanity only so far as I am one who is intrinsically able to love whatever can be loved.*
>
> PAUL WEISS, "Love in a Machine Age"

When our hands touched, my darling, suddenly I heard
the ticking of tinny tales, and the only words
left in the room were ours. I looked, and the hard
lights of twelve new machines turned on me and stared.
My friends, my dears, my fellow sufferers
of pulse and gland were gone. These things shed tears
in digits, only the randomizer behind their square
visages made them wander like us, but by wires.

Then, love, for a moment I was lonely. And I knew that pleasures
were up to us. We must taste for those lost others,
consider the rounded world, and kiss among pure
meters preoccupied with heat and pressure.

When, coming closer together, we walked in the streets,
my arm in yours, I heard the noise above my heartbeat
of a hundred roller-skaters, and when I let
my eyes turn from your learning look, only great
steel crates were moving around us. Those strangers in the city
buzzed through their memory banks for some clues to how we
stood, and without a click of analogy
roared by, unprogrammed for such leaning, love's oddity.

And then I understood, dear, that we two were the last
of the sweet speeders, body-snatchers, in a burst
and rush of joy before dark, before all the rest
wheel themselves coldly over our inconstant dust.

My cheek on your cheek, I could never have opened my eyes,
but I heard the whole globe rattle as it rolled in space,
its lands and waters stocked with metallic decoys.
We hold up history single-handed. But it says:
"Life has economies, and can't keep long, as guests
among stiff monsters, two yielding specialists.
Long before you die, chemistry will have you cast
from your little community of two kissing beasts."

So, love, I am afraid of love. Out of the corner of my eye
I watch for us to come uncoupled, for the dread day
when the clinch breaks, we step apart, and are free
to befriend those back to their humanity

who look at us now and see a robot pair
with sensors and effectors clamped together,
claiming our consciousness with clank and whirr,
delivering such data to each other,
that all uncoded comments lose their brightness.
Watt after watt compels us in our kiss,
and men, whose soft veins harden, envy us
our burning circuits, our immortal stress.

PLACET EXPERIRI

*"A 96-year-old woman was granted an interlocutory
decree of divorce yesterday and said, 'I'll never trust
another man as long as I live.' "*

THE ST. LOUIS POST-DISPATCH

To imagine it, to believe it, bring to mind all
that you know of hours and weeks when the speeches fell
on deaf ears, stuffed with suspense or fury, or the wool-
gathering eyes went blind from fluff. Bring to mind what you
    know
of love that repeats, like songs on the radio,
or of trips when the scenery came either too fast or too slow.

Even thinking of a young gardener who wastes the sense
of his first crocus in waiting to see his first quince,
then rose, then aster, though this only happens once,
will help. A year is gone. Only ninety-five
are left to account for. On the way West, one grave
to the mile, almost, will tell us how much doesn't live

to look back at what it's been through on terrible journeys.
There *are* such journeys. Something of feeling dies,
I swear it dies. And remember that even those
who got to Utah, or beyond, went three miles a day.
What kind of a map could an ant make of a city?
"I'm still alive," is about all they could say,

"the whole point was to get somewhere, and it took some time.
The new life is here, I start now. Nothing is the same."
And as for self-knowledge, everything's slow to strike home.
Give twenty years—twenty-five?—for this sort of thing,
and add that once-in-an-earth-time childhood, a long
unbroken spell of luck in a long morning.

There are plays that don't count, on shipboard and in schools,
and in cracks and corners of the world, unlucky fools
whose daydreams never come true, are never rehearsals.
At forty and fifty the organs of love say my darling,

my darling as sweetly as ever, but they know what is coming.
We must try to explain a hundred years of spring.

There are people who are slow learners and don't know it.
Remember the psychiatrist's story. All his sweat
trying to help a girl, and no go. She sat
one hour a day with hardly a word. Years passed.
He nearly gave up, but the patient said at last,
"I'm getting a lot, but please don't go so fast."

Or consider weeks of bereavement, blank mind,
locked memory. And hours of love when the stunned
ox of a lover circles around a touched hand,
or hypnotizes himself by thinking the name,
the name only, of the other. These too can come
under causes of retardation, being dumb time.

Novels never really happen, and jet flights go
too fearless, too far from the landscape—but no! NO.
Up to seventy, perhaps, but no more. Remember now
a movie scene where the cocky young surgeon repairs
his old mentor, but too carefully, and the heart tires
and stops. He begins to squeeze it, and then one hears

outrageous squeaks of the old muscle, tough
as harness leather. He squeezes and squeezes while the staff
weeps. His wet arm bulges as he works the stiff
thing in his hand with all his strength, but it dies.
What is hard and made, what has clutched and spent every juice,
ends in a rough repetition, but ends painless.

There are plants that, in the hot season, rest
and refill their bulbs. Even without care, they last.
But my God, a *heart*, aflutter in its withered chest—
Think of it, imagine it. Ninety-six years, and the world's
never opened its shell before, oyster without pearls,
insane, obscene, as pink and soft as a girl's.

AN ANNUAL AND PERENNIAL PROBLEM

> *"Among annuals and perennials, there are not many that can properly be classed among these* Heavy *and* frankly seductive *odors. No gardener should plant these in quantities near the house, or porch, or patio without realizing that many of them, in spite of exquisite fragrance, have a past steeped in sin."*
> Taylor's Garden Guide

One should have known, I suppose, that you can't even trust
the lily-of-the-valley, for all it seems so chaste.

The whole lily family, in fact, is "brooding and sultry."
It's a good thing there's a Garden Guide, nothing paltry

about *their* past. Why, some are so "stinking" one expert cried,
" 'May dogs devour its hateful bulbs!' " Enough said.

We'd better not try to imagine . . . But it's hard to endure
the thought of them sitting brazenly in churches, looking pure.

The tuberose fragrance "is enhanced by dusk and becomes"
(remember, they're taken right into some people's homes,

perhaps with teen-age children around in that air!)
"intoxicating with darkness." Well, there you are.

You hear it said sometimes that in a few cases
the past can be lived down. There's no basis

for that belief—these flowers have had plenty of time.
Sinners just try to make decent folks do the same.

What we've always suspected is true. We're not safe anywhere.
Dark patios, of course—But even at our own back door

from half a block off the jasmine may try to pollute us,
and Heaven protect us all from the trailing arbutus!

THE GARDENER TO HIS GOD

"Amazing research proves simple prayer makes flowers grow many times faster, stronger, larger."
Advertisement in The Flower Grower

I pray that the great world's flowering stay as it is,
that larkspur and snapdragon keep to their ordinary size,
and bleedingheart hang in its old way, and Judas tree
stand well below oak, and old oaks color the fall sky.
For the myrtle to keep underfoot, and no rose
to send up a swollen face, I pray simply.

There is no disorder but the heart's. But if love goes leaking
outward, if shrubs take up its monstrous stalking,
all greenery is spurred, the snapping lips are overgrown,
and over oaks red hearts hang like the sun.
Deliver us from its giant gardening, from walking
all over the earth with no rest from its disproportion.

Let all flowers turn to stone before ever they begin to share
love's spaciousness, and faster, stronger, larger
grow from a sweet thought, before any daisy
turns, under love's gibberellic wish, to the day's eye.
Let all blooms take shape from cold laws, down from a cold air
let come their small grace or measurable majesty.

For in every place but love the imagination lies
in its limits. Even poems draw back from images
of that one country, on top of whose lunatic stemming
whoever finds himself there must sway and cling
until the high cold God takes pity, and it all dies
down, down into the great world's flowering.

SESTINA FOR WARM SEASONS

It has been estimated that every seven years or so the body negotiates a complete turnover of all its substance. In other words, your body does not contain a single one of the molecules that were "you" seven years ago.

JOHN PFEIFFER, The Human Brain

Mercy on us for our many birthdays.
Never again can we envy the lobster for his new room
after the molt, nor any grub his changes.
There is no water in the waterfall
that fell before. Out of the familiar face
a stranger comes to stare every seven years.

But he learns to look like us, we browbeat the years
to repeat, to repeat, and so we waste our birthdays.
Even the astronaut, whose rubber face
slews out of shape as he bursts from the old room,
prays to the wires to hold him and let him fall
back home again, braced against all his changes.

Whoever believes the mirrored world, short-changes
the world. Over and over again our years
let us reconsider, make the old molecules fall
from out of our skins, make us go burning with birthdays.
Inside us, the bombardier may shift in his room
ten times, and may, in the instant his murderous face

peels off to show no murderer there, about-face.
And the earth will say his name each time he changes
his name in mid-air, he keeps its livingroom
open to the coming and going of more years
and of more children who believe in their birthdays.
His missiles mould away and will not fall.

But we were born to love the waterfall
and not the water. By the reflected face

we know each other, never by our birthdays.
Hearts, like lobsters, hide and heal their changes,
for our first self wants itself, and teaches the years
that leak and fill, to reproduce that room.

Even the swollen heart can only make room
for one more self. Dreaming Spring from its Fall,
knee to knee, two sit there and say that years
are all outside, that such absolute face-to-face
stops the spinning story that tells of changes.
And so, my dear, I am afraid of your birthdays.

For love is against birthdays, and locks its room
of mirrors. If your heart changes it will let fall
my face, to roll away in the defacing years.

OPEN LETTER, PERSONAL

> *"Dear Mommy. I do not like you any more. You do*
> *not like my friends so I do not like you. I will be*
> *away for some months. Love, Carla."*
> Note found in the room of an eight-year-old

My friends: If thirty people gather in a room
there is no need for winter heating. For ten years
I have shared your B.T.U.'s, and I think at the same time
of all the summer evenings when fans and airconditioners
were helpless against our being together and our smoke would
    burn
each other's eyes raw. We are both better and worse
since we met. Better and worse to be warm than lonesome.

Last spring the young writer came again, and we spoke of friends.
But this time he looked at me with his doctor's eyes in his head,
hooded and light like a river turtle's, and talked of their wounds
and drives and systems of aggression, hostility and need,
until I saw them, the skeletons of big fish, stand
around him, bleached and quiet. I am not that safe, I said,
from the hands of my friends, nor are they that safe at my hands.

It is in the strain, in the reaching of the whole mind to see
what it is that is coming toward us, what we are coming toward,
as the earliest essays on Wallace Stevens' poetry
touch and retouch the lines, trying to tell, but the words
are just behind the tip of the tongue—it is there, below
knowledge, before the settled image, that the lovely, hard
poem or person is befriended. Friendship is that sweaty play.

But believe me, my friends, we are in the late essays. A decade
has used us so that when we go out, we are at home.
We know each other's gestures like a book, we can hide
nothing personal but the noises of sex and digestion and boredom,
can leave each other only when we go to bed
or to work—the canvas, the class, the court, the consultingroom,
typewriter or lab. I am trying to say our friendship is dead.

80

Surely the jig is up. We've pinned each other down.
We know which of us will like which new novel, and why,
which of us will flirt, and with whom, and how long it will go on,
which of us are jealous of what in each other, and which fake, or
    lie,
or don't shave their legs, or don't like cheese, and very soon
your smallest children will tire of naming my couch pillows,
black, white, green, lavender and brown.

And worse: I have seen you betray affection, make a fool
of your mate, and you have seen me. I've watched you cringe and
    shake
and writhe in your selves, and you have seen me in my hospital.
I have given you paper faces and they have grown lifelike,
and you have stuck on my lips in this sheep's smile.
If I could get free of you I would change, and I would choke
this stooge to death and be proud and violent for a while.

As long as the moon hides half her face we are friends of the
    moon.
As long as sight reaches through space we are fond of the star.
But there is no space, and what light is yours and what is mine
is impossible to tell in this monstrous Palomar
where each pock is plain. I cannot dry you into fishbone
essences, I have grown into your shape and size and mirror.
I think I see you on the streets of every strange town.

We know the quickest way to hurt each other, and we have
used that knowledge. See, it is here, in the joined strands
of our weaknesses, that we are netted together and heave
together strongly like the great catch of mackerel that ends
an Italian movie. I feel your bodies smell and shove
and shine against me in the mess of the pitching boat. My friends,
we do not like each other any more. We love.

A TIME OF BEES

*Love is never strong enough to find the words be-
fitting it.*

CAMUS

All day my husband pounds on the upstairs porch.
Screeches and grunts of wood as the wall is opened
keep the whole house tormented. He is trying to reach
the bees, he is after bees. This is the climax, an end
to two summers of small operations with sprays and ladders.

Last June on the porch floor I found them dead,
a sprinkle of dusty bugs, and next day a still worse
death, until, like falling in love, bee-haunted,
I swept up bigger and bigger loads of some hatch,
I thought, sickened, and sickening me, from what origin?

My life centered on bees, all floors were suspect. The search
was hopeless. Windows were shut. I never find
where anything comes from. But in June my husband's fierce
sallies began, inspections, cracks located
and sealed, insecticides shot; outside, the bees' course

watched, charted; books on bees read.
I tell you I swept up bodies every day on the porch.
Then they'd stop, the problem was solved; then they were there
     again,
as the feelings make themselves known again, as they beseech
sleepers who live innocently in will and mind.

It is no surprise to those who walk with their tigers
that the bees were back, no surprise to me. But they had
left themselves so lack-luster, their black and gold furs
so deathly faded. Gray bugs that the broom hunted
were like a thousand little stops when some great lurch

of heart takes place, or a great shift of season.
November it came to an end. No bees. And I could watch

the floor, clean and cool, and, from windows, the cold land.
But this spring the thing began again, and his curse
went upstairs again, and his tinkering and reasoning and pride.

It is the man who takes hold. I lived from bees, but his force
went out after bees and found them in the wall where they hid.
And now in July he is tearing out the wall, and each
board ripped brings them closer to his hunting hand.
It is quiet, has been quiet for a while. He calls me, and I march

from a dream of bees to see them, winged and unwinged,
such a mess of interrupted life dumped on newspapers—
dirty clots of grubs, sawdust, stuck fliers, all smeared
together with old honey, they writhe, some of them, but who
    cares?
They go to the garbage, it is over, everything has been said.

But there is more. Wouldn't you think the bees had suffered
enough? This evening we go to a party, the breeze
dies, late, we are sticky in our old friendships and light-headed.
We tell our funny story about the bees.
At two in the morning we come home, and a friend,

a scientist, comes with us, in his car. We're going to save
the idea of the thing, a hundred bees, if we can find
so many unrotted, still warm but harmless, and leave
the rest. We hope that the neighbors are safe in bed,
taking no note of these private catastrophes.

He wants an enzyme in the flight-wing muscle. Not a bad
thing to look into. In the night we rattle and raise
the lid of the garbage can. Flashlights in hand,
we open newspapers, and the men reach in a salve
of happenings. I can't touch it. I hate the self-examined

who've killed the self. The dead are darker, but the others have
moved in the ooze toward the next moment. My God

83

one half-worm gets its wings right before our eyes.
Searching fingers sort and lay bare, they need
the idea of bees—and yet, under their touch, the craze

for life gets stronger in the squirming, whitish kind.
The men do it. Making a claim on the future, as love
makes a claim on the future, grasping. And I, underhand,
I feel it start, a terrible, lifelong heave
taking direction. Unpleading, the men prod

till all that grubby softness wants to give, *to give.*

TO SEE, TO TAKE
1970

I

"Time that is intolerant . . ."

OUTLANDISH AGON

There was something obscene about wrestling that baby-faced
    boy.
Women don't usually wrestle, except for a comic or grotesque
    effect,
but this was a fight for my life—I recognized him instantly.
I keep thinking how it must have looked, with him half my
    height,
and so slippery with sweat I couldn't keep hold, even with my
    nails,
and I'd hold his head back by the curls so he couldn't reach my
    own hair.
Once when we were locked together on the floor, his face
was right under mine. I looked into his tea-colored eyes
and saw clear through them to the blank bottom of the teacup.
It startled me so much I let go and rolled away,
and then he rolled on top of me. I felt his little genitalia pressing,
cool, and hard as marble. It was only for a moment.
What was dreadful was catching glimpses of freckles and a cute
    nose,
and dimples at the base of each fat, fierce finger.

My life—it was all I could have wanted, after I left home.
I held my spotted wand before the copulating world,
and it threw forth images ring-straked, speckled and grisled.
I believed in the power of words, both birthright and blessing.
I'd make a name for myself sooner or later,
and I could trust the men in my life to sit tight on household
    matters;
in some ways they are more domestic than women.

I was surprised at my own endurance. At one point I felt
the gristle of his nose give in under my palm and his eyelids
leak under my gouging nails. I would have killed him then,
really and truly killed him once and for all,
if I could have. But he got loose a little and somehow touched me.

Outlandish Agon

A long time ago I'd felt intimations of that strength,
in my mother's obsessed preference, her almost professional
   tricks,
in my father's preempted eyes, which couldn't meet my eyes.

Have you ever really fought all night? All that I'd call fight
took place in the first half hour. The rest of the time
we were only clutching and wiggling a little, and even so
I don't quite know how I managed to hang on.
Now that it's over I am blessed, if you can call it that,
and the shrivelled world squeaks in rust or pain when it moves.
His strength—I can't describe it—it was not muscular,
in fact he felt soft under the sweat, like soft rubber.
But I believe in his power, beyond the power of words,
beyond himself even, flexed in my own belief.

A CHRISTMAS CARD, AFTER THE ASSASSINATIONS

What is to be born already fidgets in the stem,
near where the old leaves loosened, resembling them,
or burns in the cell, ready to be blue-eyed,
or, in the gassy heavens, gathers toward a solid,
except for that baby mutant, Christ or beast,
who forms himself from a wish, our best or last.

CAUSES

"Questioned about why she had beaten her spastic child to death, the mother told police, 'I hit him because he kept falling off his crutches.'" NEWS ITEM

Because one's husband is different from one's self,
the pilot's last words were "Help, my God, I'm shot!"
Because the tip growth on a pine looks like Christmas tree candles,
cracks appear in the plaster of old houses.

And because the man next door likes to play golf,
a war started up in some country where it is hot,
and whenever a maid waits at the bus-stop with her bundles,
the fear of death comes over us in vacant places.

It is all foreseen in the glassy eye on the shelf,
woven in the web of notes that sprays from a trumpet,
announced by a salvo of crackles when the fire kindles,
printed on the nature of things when a skin bruises.

And there's never enough surprise at the killer in the self,
nor enough difference between the shooter and the shot,
nor enough melting down of stubs to make new candles
as the earth rolls over, inverting billions of houses.

"THE WISH TO BE BELIEVED"

It is never enough to know what you want.
The brick in your hand, dampened but solid, crumbles,
and a boundary being built, in the midst of building,
stops. (Why shouldn't one say what it is like?
How would they ever know, otherwise?)

You find in your pocket a key, two keys,
one with a curlicued stem, heavy, absurd,
the other perfectly blank, anonymous.
Who knows what they open; you glance at keyholes.
It is like—you can't, after all, say exactly.

And the rooms, supposing you enter them calmly,
are different from your own; one is bare,
with a gilt-framed mirror facing the door.
Suppose you are tempted to insert your face—
you see a face, and the door closing.

And you go on past the half-built boundary,
clicking the keys together, entering.
And you reach, finally, a plain, absolute place,
and stand in the center, saying to someone,
"Believe. Believe this is what I see."

FIRST FLIGHT

"What we do not wholly possess, is that what we love?"

I

Over forty years, and I haven't left your weather.
Pocketed like a new-born kangaroo,
I've sucked the dark particular.

This morning the road to the airport, sinking in snow,
seems nevertheless to ascend, bearing a birdbrain
whose will leads up, whose life tries to follow.

World, grandmother whose ghost stories made me run,
I think I've expressed my fondness for you before.
Under those scary sheets is a dear one.

Roommate, I hold my face over your popcorn-popper
as long as I can before I board the plane.
Your white rebuffs, never stormier,

strike eyelids closing to domestic vision.
Chiller, you roll out of my sight like a snowball
and I hop to meaningless sunshine.

I I

Where am I? Quick, check the old bag
for the old baggage it feels too light to bear.
Eyes, breath, heart, are you here?

The souvenir I wanted to bring fell
seconds ago, an armload of whitened antennae,
signboards, washlines and a soap factory
just the right size, I would have held them all.

So you live *here*, then, my foreigner . . .

And now I can look. Oh Lord, why didn't you tell me,
you I guessed at, how serious, how beautiful it is,
that speechlessness below, a sleeping sea,
where, kissing its frost, endlessly, everywhere,
fallen, uttering, one angel voice, desire,
fills the air with light, the perfect blasphemy.

I I I
My useless education drops away.
Old paths I wore over foothills
of A&P pushcarts, a hospital door, pencils,
polish and Simplicity patterns
will clutter shut. I ran them daily
up to a classroom mesa where, greedy,
exhilarated, shivering in thin
air, I intended to learn.

Where someone said,
"I know you love me, I feel safe with you."
What did I save her from? She's dead.

Where I played for years with someone under the moon,
bouncing his joyous, pink, four-chambered ball.
But once when I caught it and lifted it to throw,
its blood in ghastly maypole
streamers ran down my arm. An eclipse.
And even as my arm turned numb, goose-pimpled white,
what could I do but hold it tight?
My foolish fingers weakened less and less,
but we barely lived through that interval of darkness.

Where into someone's pocket I slipped,
like a compact at a dance, for luck,
my little hoard, unlit,
of imagined celebration.
What lit it? Suddenly he burned.

Rocket, sparkler, pinwheel
tore at his side like fiends and
chewed his cheek.
Those screams were ours. He didn't scream,
but turned like an incandescent top.
No one could stop it,
but I would have given a life to make it stop.

Where someone liked my jokes, and I liked his.
But God of Love, what kind of joke is this?
I held his hand once, knowing it was the last time,
and that cold hand never lets go of mine.

And all the rest.
Oh, we learned, didn't we, tricky thing in the breast?

IV

The ghosts of night are joining us, shade by shade,
walking unscathed over a burning striation
until it is covered with their cool feet.

The faces around me turn toward me,
beaming, incomprehensible lamps,
saying the stranger is the best beloved.
Oddly and without consequence, I am lighted.

If the poem were to speak without its syllables,
and love's spirit step out of its skin of need,
I would tremble like this.

V

Up front, someone deals with intricacies.
I fumble for his hands.
The plane, turning from spaciousness,

will be brought down by whoever believes
earth's the right place.
Don't tell me it is I.

VI

There is no mercy in a world
that chooses this tapestry to hang.
French knots of a monomaniac
riddle the linen, red, yellow and green,
electric, without reference, without movement.
The shocked imagination tries to enter it.

It is in honor of a reunion.
Having considered dearness in its several lights,
gray scholar in a second childhood,
tipsy, tangled in a dangle of diamonds,
too dizzy to call anything by its name,
I resent this gravity.

When I touch you I know what I'm doing.
Nothing is inconsequential.
Gatsby is dead in his swimming pool.
Stupid children chart the wood with breadcrumbs.
I believe you in everything except
the smoothness of this diminishing.

I fall into your arms of towers and foliage.
At the little bump of heart on heart
you begin to tell me I couldn't have lived without you.
I look into your hard eyes
since I am home and all is forgiven,
but liar, love, I see you against the sky.

LEDA

"Did she put on his knowledge with his power
Before the indifferent beak could let her drop?"

Not even for a moment. He knew, for one thing, what he was.
When he saw the swan in her eyes he could let her drop.
In the first look of love men find their great disguise,
and collecting these rare pictures of himself was his life.

Her body became the consequence of his juice,
while her mind closed on a bird and went to sleep.
Later, with the children in school, she opened her eyes
and saw her own openness, and felt relief.

In men's stories her life ended with his loss.
She stiffened under the storm of his wings to a glassy shape,
stricken and mysterious and immortal. But the fact is,
she was not, for such an ending, abstract enough.

She tried for a while to understand what it was
that had happened, and then decided to let it drop.
She married a smaller man with a beaky nose,
and melted away in the storm of everyday life.

THE CREATION

Now that I know you are gone
I have to try, like Rauschenberg,
to rub out, line by line,
your picture, feeling as I rub
the maker's most inhuman
joy, seeing as I rub
the paper's slow, awful return
to possibility.
Five times you screamed and won
from your short body a big boy
or a tall girl to join
the rest of us here,
and now let daughter or son
wear all that's left of your face
when this drawing's undone.

It is hard, heavy work.
The pencil indented the grain
of the paper, and I scour
a long time on a cheekbone
that doesn't want to disappear,
hoping my fingers won't learn
its line from going over and over
it. I replace your chin
with dead white.
Once, in a little vain
coquettishness, you joined
your party late, hair down
to your waist, and let the men
watch you twist it around
to a blonde rope and pin
the richness of its coils
into a familiar bun.
And now I make you bald
with my abrasion.

The hours we had to drink
before you'd put the dinner on!
My eraser's wet with sweat
as it moves on a frown
of long, tipsy decision:
were we all so drunk
it didn't matter, or should you strain
the Mornay sauce?
Already we are worn,
the eraser and I, and we
are nearing your eyes. Your garden
was what you saw each morning,
and your neighbor's, making fun
of her oversolicitude:
"I swear that woman
digs her plants up every day
to see if their roots have grown."
You tucked the ticklish roots
of half-grown youngsters, back in
and pressed the tilth around them.
Your eyes were an intervention.
You saw your words begin
a moody march to the page
when you tried to write what you'd seen
in poems you brought out one by one
to show us, getting braver
slowly—yes, too slowly. When
you finally sent some off—
too slowly—a magazine
took one and printed it
too slowly; you had just gone.
If I raise my head from this work
what I see is that the sun
is shining anyway,
and will continue to shine
no matter whose pale Dutch blue
eyes are closed or open,

no matter what graphite memories
do or do not remain,
so I erase and don't
look up again.
When I answer the phone
I don't any longer expect
your jerky conversation—
one funny little comment,
then silence until I began
trying to fill it myself;
at last the intention
would appear, "Come for dinner
and help me entertain
someone I'm scared of." It was hard
to believe you were often
really sick and afraid.
You heard the tune
of our feelings, I think,
over the phone, even.
You liked a joke.
You loved Beethoven.
And this is the end of your ear.
I see your nose redden
with summer allergies,
wrinkle at your husband's pun
and then straighten and fade.
What is left of you is graven,
almost, into one kind of smile.
I don't think I can mourn
much more than I already have
for this loved irritant—prune
pucker, with ends of lips
pulled up. More than your grin
it lasts, and with it lasts
a whole characterization
I can't dispose of
unless I rub clear through and ruin

this piece of anti-art.
When our repartee would run
too fast, or someone's anecdote
run long, or someone mention
a book you hadn't read,
that smile meant you were hidden.
It meant you needed time
to think of something clever or mean,
or that you thought we'd gone too far
from the gentle and sane.
It meant you were our wise,
dear, vulnerable, human
friend, as true and false as life
would let you be, and when
I move you that much farther from
your self to generalization
there is a blur
and your smile stops. This thing is done.

Swept empty by a cyclone
inside, I lift the paper.
But before I blow it clean,
sketched now in rubber crumbs,
another face is on it—mine,
Sneak, Poet, Mon-
ster, trying to rob you with words.

Your death was your own.

THE PIETÀ, RHENISH, 14TH C., THE CLOISTERS

He stares upward at a monstrous face,
as broad as his chest, as long as he is
from the top of his head to his heart. All her
feeling and fleshiness is there.

To be on her lap is to be all shrunken
to a little composition of bone
and held away from her upper body,
which, like an upended cot smoothed neatly

and topped with a tight, girlish bolster
of breasts, rises behind him, queer
to them both, as if no one had ever rested
upon it, or rumpled it, or pressed it.

And so it stands free of suffering.
But above it, the neck, round and wrinkling
from the downward tilt of the head it's bearing,
bears the full weight of that big thing.

It is a face that, if he could see
as we are forced to see, and if he
knew, as we cannot help but know, that
his dead, dangling, featureless, granite

feet would again have to touch the ground,
would make him go mad, would make his hand,
whose hard palm is the same size
as one of his mother's tearless eyes,

hit it, since nothing in life can cure
pain of this proportion. To see her
is to understand that into the blast
of his agony she turned, full-faced,

and the face began to melt and ache,
the brows running down from their high arc
to the cheekbone, the features falling toward the chin,
leaving the huge forehead unlined, open,

until, having felt all it could feel,
her face numbed and began to congeal
into this. With horror he'd have to see
the massive girl there, vapidly

gazing, stupid, stupefied.
If he said, "Willingly I dried
out of consciousness and turned to the slight
husk you hold on your knee, but let

an innocent, smaller love of a son
hold me, let not my first stone
be the heart of this great, grotesque mother.
Oh God, look what we've done to each other,"

then from the head her slow wit,
stirring, would speak, "My darling, it was not
I who belittled you, but love
itself, whose nature you came to believe

was pure possibility, though you came through
its bloody straits. And not you,
but love itself, has made me swell
above you, gross and virginal

at once. I touch what's left on my knee
with the tips of my fingers—it is an ugly,
cold corrugation. Here on my lap,
close in my arms, I wanted to keep

both the handsome, male load of your whole
body and the insupportable,
complete weightlessness of your loss.
The holy and incestuous

met and merged in my love, and meet
in every love, and love is great.
But unmanned spirit or unfleshed man
I cannot cradle. Child, no one can."

A DAY IN LATE OCTOBER

for Randall Jarrell

I

It is time to drive in the hills
and look at leaves,
time to envision again
the fortunate fall of light,
which must have come down this week
like a snow of angels.
Angel after angel lies with his chosen
fat little earthy color.
In those thousand thousand embraces
no one can see now
who corrupts and who illuminates. . . .

I I

"If Galileo had said in verse that the earth moved,
the Inquisition might have let him alone"—so Hardy
turned from the mighty fictions. "I too dislike it. There are things
important . . ." laying her hand on the granite block of a library,
a beautiful old woman said simply, "It's cool to my hand."
Five poets live in the open ward of a Midwest city
where the paper's book page editor snorts, "Review that stuff?
That stuff's been dead for fifty years," each with his goofy,
compulsive tricks to keep from thinking, "What if it's true?"
A poet in his cups at one of those Washington, D.C.
meetings said, "It's a bunch of black marks. The rest is the
    reader's
love, goodwill or foolishness." Less and less do we
know what it is. Like the Bushmen who want to be left in peace,
one of its names would seem to be *Twa*, meaning "only" or
    "merely."

III
The helpless tribe in Iowa
could neither beat nor conjure
its little savage into line.
That child would scream at beasts,
at cows who lifted gaunt faces
to feast their bulged, hallucinating eyes
on her. When the corn grew over her head,
Reform School boys broke out
and hid in the cornrows till dark.
She hid with them. Her hand sweated
with theirs on the blooded lug wrench,
but she didn't hop the freight.
The grotesque stretched lips of friends,
the parental faces striped with clay and dung
scared her to death.
Later, reading the anthropologists,
all these became familiar.
I tell you I read that stuff for dear life.

IV
All my Quixotes, gentle Dons,
reading your books for days,
I think how the mad world turns golden
under your foolish eyes,

and of how your world once held me
and holds me still.
Those windmills would have killed me.
I believe we are real.

V
Hidden in his *emploi de temps*
is the actuality of another's life.
Over and over time goes wrong,
leaves us stuck below zero in grief,

tolls its unearthly, unbearable ding-dong,
takes the tree and leaves the leaf.

Because the human calendar
can't count more than a single spring,
can't teach even the most brilliant year
to come back twice from its wintering,
when a poet dies in late October
we learn nothing from nature, nothing.

VI
. . . Later the throats of sidewalks back home
will rasp and tickle,
be cleared,
then rasp and tickle again
until the cold they're always getting
settles in every larynx, and each forgets
what it was he wanted to say.

Before that happens, I want to say no bright or seasonal thing,
only that there is too much the incorruptible poem refuses to
swallow. At the end of each line, a clench of teeth and something
falling away—tasteless memory, irreducible hunk of love, unbelievably bitter repetition, rancid failure at feeling and naming.
And the poem's revulsions become a lost world, which also contains what cannot be imagined: your death, my death.

ADVICE TO A GOD

Before you leave her, the woman who thought you lavish,
whose body you led to parade without a blush
the touching vulgarity of the *nouveau-riche*,

whose every register your sexual coin
crammed full, whose ignorant bush mistook for sunshine
the cold, brazen battering of your rain,

rising, so little spent, strange millionaire
who feels in his loins' pocket clouds of power
gathering again for shower upon golden shower,

say to her, since she loves you, "Those as unworldly
as you are fated, and I can afford, to be
may find in Love's bed the perfect economy,

but, in all of his other places, a populace
living in fear of his management, his excess
of stingy might and extravagant helplessness.

Turn from him, Danae. I am greater by far,
whose flower reseeds without love for another flower,
whose seas part without loneliness, whose air

brightens or darkens heartlessly. By chance
I have come to you, and a progeny of events,
all that the mind of man calls consequence,

will follow my coming, slaughter and marriage, intrigue,
enchantment, definition of beauty, hag
and hero, a teeming, throwaway catalogue

of the tiniest, riskiest portion of my investment.
Yet pity your great landlord, for if I lent
so much as an ear to you, one loving tenant,

your bankrupt scream as I leave might tempt me to see
all creation in the ungainly, ungodly
throes of your individuality."

II

"Heut' oder morgen kommt der Tag,
And how shall we bear it?

Lightly, lightly."

HOMEWORK

for Jim

Lest the fair cheeks begin their shrivelling
before a keeping eye has lit on their fairness,
I pluck from the stony world some that can't cling
to stone, for a homely, transparent form to bless.

Smothering Elbertas, if not Albertines,
in the thick, scalding sweetness of my care,
I add a touch of tart malice, some spicy scenes
and stirring, and screw the lid on love's breathless jar.

There in a frieze they stand, and there they can stay
until, in the fickle world's or the jaded heart's
hunger for freshness, they are consumed away.
Oh I know, I know that, great or humble, the arts

in their helplessness can save but a few selves
by such disguises from Time's hideous bite,
and yet, a sweating Proust of the pantry shelves,
I cupboard these pickled peaches in Time's despite.

EROS TO HOWARD NEMEROV

It's funny, Howard, I never thought I'd be
exposed at a poetry reading. All this time
my best disguises have been run up in rhyme.
My capriciousness and downright perversity

are what poets usually give as the reasons why
I appear as a babe. You took another look,
and, bare though I've always been, it came as a shock
to be seen with so clear and literal an eye.

You told those kids you thought my compelling power
comes from the fact that I stand for the unborn child
who wants to be born, and my slyness, my rage, my wild
scheming and cruelty serve that blind desire.

The youngsters will soon forget it, I'll see to that,
in the gorgeous fury and mindlessness of love,
but with you, a father and a maker of poems that have
more balance, more reticence than some, I thought

I'd have this little chat to let you know
I'm as busy as ever this fruitful year of the mini
and the marijuana. I've never been able to afford any
scruples, but I'd like to tell you you're right, my bow

still shoots for the sweetest dream the human creature
can have, the dream of possibility.
My Hippie babies, conceived in LSD,
crawl through the woods and streets, and human nature,

in their dirty faces and their beautiful bare behinds,
is carried along as ever. Every nation
is afraid of explosions of atoms or population,
but I count on you to say I've enough on my hands

without taking the larger view; that other gods
who watch other things and who often get in my way
(though if I were a mortal I'd invoke them night and day—
Demeter, for instance, could do much more with *her* seeds)

must get off their butts and help at the labs and polls.
I'll keep life coming—they'll have to keep it alive—
and to do my stuff I'll use what I can of the jive
and jazz and Beatles and bennies and Twiggy girls.

But first I owe you, I guess, one glimpse at the state
of my affairs as I see them. Let's take San Francisco:
Out on the campuses things are going so-so—
nude-in or love-in, it's what is going to come out

that I'm most concerned with, naturally, and signs
are no substitute for siblings. But homefolks do well,
considering that getting home is all uphill,
and downtown I'm not discouraged by waiting lines

of tourists who come to see the transvestite bars,
then go back and blunt my arrows on The Pill.
There are people on Broadway who are my people still,
I'm still in business, I have my entrepreneurs,

and still well-filled is a bar I specially prize,
where, setting down drink after drink like a daughter of Lot,
their star attraction, The Topless Mother of Eight,
dangles her golden dugs before men's eyes.

A QUIET AFTERNOON AT HOME

Not exactly disembodied, but speaking from no mouth,
oracular, or at least cryptic—even the dog
snaps to baffled attention, his head on one side—in eloquent in-
    flections, with quite a range of feelings,
low-pitched, but rising sometimes to an almost feminine whine,
the voice of the stomach, or thereabouts, sounds in the room,
saying perhaps, Go and ask yourself whether
there is not too much roughage in the world these days.
All these upheavals and revolutions are not without cause, you
    know.
No one is perfect, granted. But you may have forgotten
that it is entirely possible to have guts and be sensitive
at the same time. Or, in more plaintive tones,
My dear ones, I've seldom been so upset. I really can't hold my
    peace
a moment longer. Call it a virus abroad in the land,
call it a poisonous, toxic miasma creeping
around the globe if you like. That will help nothing.
O, go back to the simple things. Remember the milk of human
    kindness.
Or, It is good to be reminded that not everything can be put into
    words.
The deepest syllables sound in our juices and wellsprings.
Or, there is a strong tendency in people connected with the arts
to be taken in by appearances, to swallow anything.
Are they all that innocent? Might I suggest, rather, gluttonous?
Or perhaps not saying any of these things at all.
Perhaps only speaking up for a more visceral poetry.

BILLINGS AND COOINGS FROM "THE BERKELEY BARB" (*Want-Ad Section*)

. . . Couples sought (enclose photographs please)
by couple who've expeditiously run through
(and are eager for permutations *a quatre, a seize*)
all known modes of the sweet conjunction for two.

Gay guy needs, for a few conventional
dances and such, fem Lez to pose as date,
in return for which she can really have a ball
with her butch friend at parties he'll give in private.

How bright the scholars who use a previous schooling
to get the further enlightenment they want!
Well-rounded girl will do it hung from the ceiling
by ropes in exchange for a used copy of Kant.

A youth who pines in his present incarnation
but remembers with pleasure being a parakeet
seeks a girl just as reluctantly human
and formerly budgerigar, for a mate.

At Blank's bar, woman who'd like the *frisson*
of sex with an ex-guru should ask for Gus.
An A.C.-D.C. will share pad with someone
similarly ambidextrous.

Boy seeks cute girlfriend to share his sack
How startling now the classic or pastoral!
and lists his qualifications to attract:
"tall, dark, sensitive, handsome, sterile."

Student who can't remember the phone number
or the face of student he met at Jack's last fall,
but can't forget the hard nipples, would like her
to dial xx (transvestites need not call).

Delights they probably never knew they could have
nineteen-year-old will guarantee to disclose
to women between fifty and sixty-five
with unusually big feet or long toes.

How dazzling love's infinite variety!
How fertile is nature in her forms of joy!
Male seeks, in the area around Berkeley,
another male whose fetish is corduroy . . .

BIRTHDAY CARD FOR A PSYCHIATRIST

Your friends come fondly to your living room
believing, my dear, that the occasion's mild.
Who still feels forty as a moral *crise*
in this, the Century of the Common Child?

Uncommon gifts, brought to mid-life in pain,
are not a prize. The age demands a cure
for tragedy and gives us brand-new charts
for taking down our psychic temperature.

Othello, of course, regrets having been aggressive,
Hamlet feels pretty silly to think he trusted
terms such as "art" and "honor" instead of "projection,"
and out on the moor King Lear feels maladjusted.

An arrogant richness of the human stuff
is not a value. Nobody wants to be
left holding the bag of himself when all the others
are a democratic homogeneity.

Prospero strips down to his underpants
to teach Miranda that fathers can be informal,
while Cleopatra, Juliet, Rosalind, Kate
fight for the golden apple labelled NORMAL.

In such a state, what laurels can poems bring,
what consolation, what wishes, what advice?
May your conflicts thin out with your hair? BE HAPPY?
We hope you're feeling well? We think you're nice?

Till Burnam Wood shall come to Dunsinane,
till time shall tell us what we really are,
till Responsibility, not Health, defines
the terms of living on this serious star.

to receive the trauma of birth and pass it on
is all we're here for. Yet we hope you realize
we're glad that forty years ago you came
to join in our neurotic enterprise.

FOOTNOTES TO THE AUTOBIOGRAPHY OF BERTRAND RUSSELL

for Viktor

I

"(we did not go to bed the first time we were lovers, as there was too much to say.)"

Once out of Eden, love learned its deviousness
and found in Word its wiliest metaphor;
so if a heart, untouched and in rich disguise,
using the lips to speak of weather and war,

should receive from another masquerading heart
conversing of war and weather, the news of its need,
both may be tempted by art for the sake of art.
A long-winded discourse no other member can read,

page after page on weather and war, may ensue,
they think, with margins of blank sophistication.
And should the pedantic body scrawl there, "How true!"
dumfounded lovers can continue the conversation.

II

"Her objections to [marrying] him are the following: (a) He sleeps with 7 dogs on his bed. She couldn't sleep a wink in such circumstances. (b) . . ."

This seems, in a world where love must take its chances,
undue distaste for the first of its circumstances.

What in so snug a sleeper could be more rare
than to sense in so snuggling a crowd something lacking there?

And it seems that the lady lacks sensitivity
to how brilliant her hymeneal reception might be:

First, on the heated bed he'd push aside
seven drowsing dogs to insert one blushing bride,

and surely all other nuptial welcome pales
before a sweet thrashing given her by seven tails!

Fourteen ears attuned to their master's voice
would attend the orisons of their master's choice

in bitches, and should some Donne-reading flea propose
a speedy union, he'd suffer twenty-eight paws.

Garlanded, guarded, graced with panting devotion,
the human pair would partake of wedded emotion,

she with unwinking eyes on the dogs, and he
jostling dogs with his old impunity

until, under his lips, her eyelids would close
and the dear beast of the heart come to discompose

the bed whereon seven pairs of canine eyes
would gaze at each other with a wild surmise.

IN THE COLD KINGDOM

> *"The younger brother roasted a breast of Pishiboro's*
> *elephant wife and handed Pishiboro some, which he*
> *presently ate. Then the younger brother said in a*
> *voice full of scorn. 'Oh you fool. You lazy man. You*
> *were married to meat and you thought it was a*
> *wife.'"* FROM A MYTH OF THE BUSHMEN

Poised upside down on its duncecap,
a shrunken purple head,
True Blueberry,
enters its tightening frame of orange lip,
and the cream of a child's cheek is daubed with
Zanzibar Cocoa, while
  Here at the Martha Washington
  Ice Cream Store
  we outdo the Symbolistes.
a fine green trickle—
Pistachio? Mint Julep?
  Words have colors,
  and colors are tasty.
sweetens his chin.
In front of me Licorice teeters like a lump of coal
on its pinkish base of Pumpkin.
  A Rauschenberg tongue
  fondles this rich donnée,
  then begins to erase it.

Turning from all that is present
in the flesh, so to speak,
let the eye wander off to a menu,
where it can start to ingest
"Quite Sour Lemon sherbet,
topped with a stem cherry and chocolate sprinkles
  Swilling in language,

all floating in bubbly cherry phosphate
the bloated imagination
is urged to open still wider
and shovel it in,
and served with a twist of pretzel."
In this world "Creamy Vanilla and
Smooth Swiss Chocolate ice creams"
can be "blended with chopped pineapple,
dark fudge sauce, ripe bananas, whipped topping,
cookies, roasted nutmeats and nippy chopped cherries."
the Unconscious, that old hog,
being in charge here of the
creative act.

At about the moment my tastebuds
receive a last tickle of Gingersnap
and begin to respond to
Orange Fudge, I look at you
who have bought my ice cream cones for twenty years,
Moving another new ice to the mouth
we needn't remember
and look away
it is always the same mouth
that melts it.
My mind assembles a ribald tower
of sherbet dips, all on one cone,
Apricot, Apple, Tangerine, Peach, Prune, Lime,
and then it topples.
You are steadier than I.
You order one dip always,
or, in a dish, two dips of the same flavor.

In this hysterical brilliance of neon
Come on, consumers,
we've got to keep scooping
it is twelve or fifteen of us
to thirty ice creams.
so that the creams shall not rise
like cold lava out of their bins,
numbing our feet, our knees,
freezing our chests, our chins, our eyes,
Open the door, quick,
and let in two handholding adolescents.
Coping with all those glands
makes them good and hungry.
so that, flying out of their cannisters,
the chopped nuts
shall not top off our Technicolor grave
with their oily ashes.

Listen! All around us toothsome cones
are suffering demolition
down to the last, nipple-like tip.
How do we know where to stop?
Perhaps the glasses and dishes
are moulded of candy, and the counters and windows . . .
Over your half-eaten serving of Italian Delight,
why are you looking at me
the way you are looking at me?

POSTCARDS FROM CAPE SPLIT

I
"What is that flower?" we asked right away. What a sight!
From the rocks of the beach all the way up the hill to our house,
and all around the house and on either side of the road,
a solid ocean of flowers, shifting in the wind, shifting
in shades of pink like strokes of a brush. Heliotrope.
Pinky-white masses of bloom on five-foot red stems.
"My father brought it here," our landlady says.
" 'Be careful of heliotrope,' they told him, 'it spreads like a
    weed.' "
It has taken the hill and the house, it is on its way down the road.
Little paths are scythed through heliotrope to the sea,
from the house to the outhouse, from the road to the house,
and a square of back yard is cut away from the flowers.
"The heliotrope is taking my raspberry patch,"
the neighbor tells us, and, snuggled in heliotrope,
the kitchen gardens fight for their viney lives,
one here, one there. You can't even see them until
you're right on their edge, leaning over the heliotrope.

II
Everything looks like the sea but the sea.
The sea looks like a lake
except when fucus is dumped on its low-tide border
like heaps of khaki laundry left out to rot—
this seems a capacity for waste that is worthy of an ocean.
But the diningroom floor looks like the sea,
wide old boards, painted dark green,
that heave and ripple in waves.
Light hits the crest of each board and gives it a whitecap.

The house saves everything,
crutches and children's sleds, painted cups without handles,

chairs without seats, dried sweetgrass, fir tips in pillows.
It must be almost as old as it looks—
the father of our seventy-year-old landlady built it.
It is buffed by the salt winds to elephant color.

One goes on vacation to housekeep another way.
I have made a chart of the tides,
which are now a part of my order for a few weeks.
I have learned the perverse ways of this house—
sink and refrigerator in the kitchen,
stove, dishes and table in the diningroom.
I have tied back white net curtains,
still creased from display in the dimestore.
I have found paths through heliotrope
to each new neighbor.

III
We move in a maze of villages—
Addison, East Addison, South Addison,
Machias, East Machias and Machiasport.
(The *ch* is pronounced *ch*, and not *k*.)
The lobsters and cheese are at South Addison,
the doctor, the bakery and the liquor store are at Machias,
the nearest post office and, they say, frozen chicken livers
are at Addison, the seafood cannery is at East Machias.
East Addison and Machiasport we have so far been able to ignore.

The kitchen in this house is papered in villages.
Five villages from floor to ceiling, I don't know how many
across the wall. There is no place to locate one's self.
Still, because the dog snores by the oilstove, the brown
sparrow-size birds squeak cheerily in a spruce by the outhouse,
little toy boats are out on the sea after lobsters, the sun
is warm and the heliotrope is blowing like waves,
because, my God, it *is* pleasant here,
we can surely live uncentered for three weeks,
gleaning a little from one village, a little from another.

I V

Who would believe that we could learn to cook, drink, bathe,
shave, fill the dog's bowl, the icecube tray, the vase
for wildflowers, and keep ourselves in clean clothes and towels
on two buckets of water a day? Of course we steam mussels
and lobsters in, drive the dog into, wade in, and gaze upon
the sea, and that saves on our freshwater needs.
Each morning we take our two buckets, go down the road
to the landlord's house, walk in the back door
(as we were told to do) and get our water
and a hot donut, or a story about the old times here.
But we want to be self-sufficient the rest of the day,
neither past nor people between us and the ocean,
and so we have learned this new skill for the summer.

But what a small thirst one has, in summer, for the everyday
    water,
whereas, for the salty stranger, from here to the horizon
at high tide is no more than we can drink in
in a single day.

v

There are thirty-five stalks of corn in our garden.
Our landlord is trying to raise some corn this year.
He has staked and tied every stalk
to hold it against the sea winds.
Our landlady dopes the tassels with liniment
to keep the raccoons off.
Except for its corn and its heliotrope wall,
our garden is just like others all over the Cape:
four rows of potatoes,
two rows of string beans,
one row each of peas and beets,
one row of squash,
and one row of dahlias.

The man from across the bar
brought us a sea-moss pudding
in a silver dish.

VI
Our landlord's youngest son, the lobsterman,
comes in his lobstering boots, turned halfway down,
to fix our oilstove. I am dazzled by the man in boots.
It is as if a heron stood in my diningroom.

His father sits in a rocker by his kitchen stove,
knitting the twine innards for lobster traps
and saying, "When we were young I'd go out in a skiff,
why, right off here, and spear a half bushel of flounder
while She cooked breakfast. We had dried fish all winter,
and they was *some good*, I tell you." The day's light changes.

We drove inland a ways, through the Blueberry Barrens.
Mile after mile, from road to the far mountains
of furzy wasteland, flat. You almost miss it.
Suddenly, under that empty space, you notice
the curious color of the ground. Blue mile, blue mile,
and then a little bent-over group of Indians
creeping down string-marked aisles. Blue mile, blue mile,
and then more Indians, pushing their forked dustpans.
It looks like a race at some country picnic, but lost
in that monstrous space, under that vacant sky.

Why am I dazzled? It is only another harvest.
The world blooms and we all bend and bring
from ground and sea and mind its handsome harvests.

A SPELL OF CONJUNCTIVITIS

The act of seeing a tree is the act of pressing
an etched eyeball against the damp paper sky,
carefully, carefully, and there it hangs, a fresh print.
An elegant frame of fur defines the start as mid-trunk
and the highest achievement as a slight tapering.
But how insistently it gathers itself together,
forcing the multitudinous scratchings out of which it is composed
into a perpendicular, a tree, recognizably sycamore.
One supposes that the three great cloudy balls
hanging from its branches like fruit are not its own,
but appeared from some imperfection of the press—
though they match the frame and seem an arty improvement.

The dog leaps through hoops of fur, disappearing for a second
into a cloud that clearly contains the fourth dimension.
He reappears with a somewhat damaged solidity,
with several legs that require an instant to rejoin their body,
and three permanent patches of light on his black hide
which may be the other side of the room shining through.

The faces of my friends are on balloons that drift and rise.
When they go through my ceiling I can only imagine how high
    they are going,
one hovering, one all pure wasteless lift,
one snagging and coming free, snagging and coming free, all the
    way up,
one swelling, perhaps, in the light air.
They bounce around me, beautiful and unfathomed,
a pirate with a gray patch on his eye,
faces with missing mouths, as if this tenderness, that kooky wit
were inexpressible. I want to touch them.
How precariously they are delivered to my senses, and with what
    loss of self-containment!

IN THE HOSPITAL FOR TESTS

My mother's friend cooked for the drunk-and-disorderlies,
and so, when I was ten, I peeked at a cell,
and that's what I'd swear this room came out of—the county jail.
But here in a sweat lies a strange collection of qualities,
with me inside it, or maybe only somewhere near it,
while all the nonsense of life turns serious again—
bowel movements, chickenpox, the date of one's first menstrua-
   tion,
the number of pillows one sleeps on, postnasal drip—
"It has very high arches," I hear the resident note.
He has worked his way down over its ridges and jerks,
its strings and moistures, coursings, lumps and networks,
to the crinkled and slightly ticklish soles of its feet.
"Don't worry, if there's anything going on here," the interne
   says,
"we'll find it. I myself have lots of ideas."

Across the room, over a jungle of plants,
blooming, drooping, withering, withered and dead,
a real face watches, freckled and flat blue eyed.
Sometimes her husband visits, a man of plaid shirts
and apologetic smiles, and sometimes three red-head
little girls in stairsteps, too scared to talk out loud.

In twenty-four hours, the hefty nurse, all smiles,
carries out my urine on her hip like a jug of cider,
a happy harvest scene. My room-mate, later,
gets on a stretcher, clutching her stomach, and it wheels
her off down the halls for a catheter in her heart.
There's one chance in five hundred she'll die in the test. She'd like
to live for two more years for the children's sake.
Her husband waits in the room. He sweats. We both sweat.

In the Hospital for Tests

She was only fifteen when they married, he says, but she told him
she was past eighteen and he didn't find out for years.
She's wheeled back, after a feverish two hours,
with black crochet on her arm. She was conscious all the time,
and could feel whatever it was, the little box, go
through her veins to the left of the chest from the right elbow.

The leukemia across the hall, the throat cancer a few doors down,
the leaky valve who has to sleep on eight pillows—
these sit on our beds and talk of the soggy noodles
they gave us for lunch, and the heat, and how long, how soon.
The room stinks of my urine and our greed.
To live, to live at all costs, that's what we want.
We never knew it before, but now we hunt
down the healthy nurses with our eyes. We gobble our food.
Intruders come from outside during visiting hours
and chatter about silly things, no longer our affairs.

"A little more blood, I'm on the trail." He'll go far,
my interne. My room-mate gets on the stretcher again;
she comes back almost dead, but they give her oxygen.
She whistles for breath, her face is swollen and sore
and dark. She spits up white rubber. The bronchoscope,
that's what it was this time, and more tests to come.
She wishes her husband had been here after this one.
They were going to do the other lung too, but they had to stop.

In the middle of the night her bed blazes white in the darkness.
Three red-headed daughters dangle from her lightcord.
The nurse holds a cup to her lips. It is absurd,
she is swallowing my poems. The air knots like a fist,
or a heart, the room presses in like a lung. It is empty
of every detail but her life. It is bright and deathly.

"You can go home this afternoon. You're all checked out."
My doctor is grinning over the obscene news.
My room-mate sits up and listens. "God only knows
what causes these things, but you've nothing to worry about."
In shame I pack my bag and make my call.
She reads a magazine while I wait for my husband.
She doesn't speak, she is no longer my friend.
We say goodbye to each other. I hope she does well.
In shame I walk past the staring eyes and their reproaches
all down the hall. I walk out on my high arches.

THE GOOD RESOLUTION

My right hand has suffered an amputation
of its fifth finger, the one with the hot nail,
the one that kept pointing across the room.
While the other four fingers sealed my lips and the thumb
asked for a hitchhike to my shoulder, it would point Away.
Now I am self-absorbed and lonesome.

Drifting in great woolly scarves in my head,
like the scene of an English thriller, a fog settles.
My head turns slowly, the fog shifts, and inside
its brow, crouched, the sweating maniac is revealed.
He froths and tightens, he starves for the white victim.
Now I am restless and in need of food.

The day extends itself, like a dog's tongue
in dreadful heat, or, like a bay bridge,
crosses ten empty islands and still keeps going.
Light dangles from the sky like a wet string.
I try to jerk it down, but it holds fast
and will not drop into interminable evening.

Who would have thought I'd be asking that old chestnut
at my age, seriously, Who Am I, demoralized
giant-killer or really furious giant?
One imagines paper dolls from a folded sheet
flipped open to a whole procession of selves, hands joined,
by this time. I can't wait and I won't cheat,

and so my simple twins lay hands on each other
and bend each other down to a compromise:
Five times daily let the screws be loosed, the failure
celebrated, and perhaps in the homely future,
tripping with a pursed mouth toward some Damascus,
I'll fall to my knees and rise up a non-smoker.

I am poured into five daily boxes, and all
my contents are fingered and re-arranged, arranged
and fingered. The screen I blow is too thin to conceal.
A mouse in the mind, trapped by its tail
in front of a mirror, keeps squeaking over and over
it never wanted to know itself *this* well!

INTO MEXICO

Past the angular maguey fields, a ride on the optic nerve,
we come to the first rest stop, and the visit begins.
It is what I have always wanted; to follow the first signs
in another language makes me weak with joy. I am brave
out back in a courtyard, by a shack that might be the toilet,
when bulging senoras bump me on the back and shoulder me.
If they look at me I do not know what they see,
since even metaphors are changed. Overhead in the heat
the skinned, outrageous body of some animal hangs from a line.
Is it rotting, or drying? I've never smelled its rawness before.
Yes, there is a stool in the shack, and soiled toilet paper
in a waist-high pile beside it. Water is in a can.

I touch the paper on the roll, it is rough, it is like . . . nothing
    else.
I am behind the eyes at last. It is as if one could by-pass
love, when the other eyes parry with a picture of one's own face,
and never arrive at marriage, either true or false,
when eyes glaze and minds are more private than ever,
but could stop in between at a point where no one
can stop. To be in one's first foreign country, in approximation,
is to be in you—or to feel what it must be like to be there.

Now it is one long agony of taking-in. From the bus
I can see inside the palings, or tin, or straw of a shelter,
and all pots, braziers and pallets are unfamiliar.
At the first market, walking in through the restless
yellow of bananas, I will go to such furnishings and handle them.
Country dogs here are yellow also, with a long body.
And all the time I have lived as if you were like me.
Now, here, I am released from that stratagem.

In the city I would never have expected a glassy hotel
to rise between little sheds of pink and orange cement,
nor men to pull down their pants and squat in the vacant
lot downtown. Sweet rolls—I am trying to taste them all,
but it will take weeks—are named for creatures and the parts
of creatures, Snails, Cheeks, Noses, Ears, Dogs.
What is that snarled bouquet of herbs a little boy drags
toward home, making a green sweep of the streets?
A woman kneels on the pavement all day to sell
six pyramids of seven cracked walnuts each.
I tongue a clay cup that tastes of dark and starch,
and buy eggs singly, since the price of one is marked on its shell.
Each noise, each name, is enchanted and necessary.
I drift in bed, astonished by faintness and nausea and chills.
I would never have felt this way—is this the way it feels?
Thousands of black beans shine near sweet potato candy.

One starves for this journey, I think, a simple sensing of what is
not thou, not it, but you—a visit behind the eyes
where the map bulges into belief, relief, presents sea,
mountains, macadam, presents a strange and willful country.

REMEDIES, MALADIES, REASONS

Her voice, that scooped me out of the games of the others
to dump me in bed at seven for twelve years,

and yelled me up to my feet if I sat on the ground,
liable to catch pneumonia, and each year penned

the feet, that wanted to walk bare, or hike
or wade, in the cramping, pygmy shoes of the chronic

invalid, intoned each time I raged or cried
the old story of how I'd nearly died

at six weeks from nursing a serum she'd taken,
so I'd never be well. Each day all over again

she saved me, pitted against rain, shine, cold, heat,
hunting in my mouth each morning for a sore throat,

laying a fever-seeking hand on my forehead
after school, incanting "Did your bowels move good?

Wrap up before you go out and don't play hard.
Are you *sure* you're not coming down with a cold? You look
    tired,"

keeping me numb on the couch for so many weeks,
if somehow a wily cough, flu or pox

got through her guard, my legs would shake and tingle,
trying to find the blessed way back to school.

Girl Scouts, green apples, tree climbs, fairs—the same
no. "But the other kids . . ." "Well, you're not like *them*."

Food was what, till I gagged, she kept poking in,
and then, with high enemas, snaked out again;

her one goose, refusing to fatten, I showed
her failure and shamed her with every bone I had.

If I screamed that I'd run away if I couldn't go,
she'd say, "All right, but that'll be the end of you,

you'll get sick and who'll pay the doctor bill?
You'll *die*, you know as well as I do you will."

I was scared to die. I had to carry a hankyful
of big white mineral pills, a new cure-all,

for months, and gulp them in classes every half hour.
They spilled on the floor in front of my favorite teacher.

A spastic went jerking by. "That's how *you'll* get
from twitching your finger all the time. Now quit it!"

A bandaged head moaned in the hospital. "Mastoid.
That's how *you'll* be if you don't stop blowing hard."

Only once, dumfounded, did she ever notice a thing
that might be thought of as strength in me. Breaking

another free yardstick from the drygoods store
on a butt and legs still bad, she found her junior

in high school fighting back till we rolled on the floor.
That night she said I wouldn't get spanked any more.

She took me to college and alerted the school nurse.
I went in without looking back. For four years

I tested each step, afraid to believe it was me
bearing like a strange bubble the health of my body

as I walked the fantastic land of the ordinary
and learned how to tear up the letters, "You *know* how I worry,

for my sake please don't do it . . . don't try it . . . don't go . . .
You *surely* wouldn't want to make me worry like I do!"

Marriage, work, books, years later, called
to help them when she and Dad both lay in bed,

I first stepped back in their house for a stay of more
than a few days. Soon she was crying "Come back here!

Don't you dare go outside that door without your sweater!"
"But it's hot out," said the innocent, visiting neighbor.

"Oh, but she's never been well, I have to keep watching
her like a hawk or she comes right down with something."

There, on my big shoulders, against such proof—
a quarter of a century of the charmed life

I'd been living outside the door—she could still see
the weak, rolling head of a death-threatened baby.

In a hundred visits and fifteen hundred letters
she's been showing herself to me for thirty years

(as well as six thousand days of retrospect)
in clear colors. I know what to expect

before I open my ears or the envelope.
She had to get up three times a night to "dope"

a sore, she "gargled and sprayed" for a week so as not
to get "what was going around." There was blood in the snot

she blew out last month. She "hawks up big gobs
of stuff" that is almost orange. All of her tubes

are blocked. Her face turned purple. Lettuce she ate
was "passed" whole, "green as grass" in the toilet.

She "came within an inch" of a "stoppage," but mineral oil
saved her from all but "a running-off of the bowel."

Sniffing her mucus or sweat or urine, she marvels
anew at how "rotten" or "rank" or "sour" it smells.

There's never been any other interesting news.
Homer of her own heroic course, she rows

through the long disease of living, and celebrates
the "blood-red" throat, the yellow pus that "squirts"

from a swelling, the taste, always "bitter as gall,"
that's "belched up," the bumps that get "sore as a boil,"

the gas that makes her "blow up tight as a drum,"
the "racing heart," the "new kind of bug," the "same

old sinus," the "god-awful cold"—all things that make
her "sick as a dog" or "just a nervous wreck."

Keeping her painstaking charts, first mariner
of such frightful seas, she logs each degree and number

("Three hundred thousand units of penicillin
he gave me last Thursday!" "I puked four times, and the last one

was *pure bile!*" "Fever way up to ninety-
nine-point-nine!") Daily, but not humbly,

she consults the eight shelves of the six-foot, steel,
crammed-with-medication oracle.

I know what she is, I know what she always was:
a hideous machine that pumps and wheezes,

suppurating, rotting, stinking, swelling,
its valves and pipes shrieking, its fluids oozing

in the open, in violent color, for students to learn
the horror, the nausea, of being human.

And yet, against all the years of vivid, never-
varying evidence, when I look at her

I see an attractive woman. And looking back,
testing the truth of a child's long-ago look,

I still see the mother I wanted, that I called to come,
coming. From the dark she rushes to my bedroom,

switching the lamp on, armed with pills, oils, drops,
gargles, liniments, flannels, salves, syrups,

waterbag, icebag. Bending over me,
giant, ferocious, she drives my Enemy,

in steamy, hot-packed, camphorated nights,
from every sickening place where he hides and waits.

Do you think I don't know how love hallucinates?

III

'Love took my hand, and smiling did reply,
  'Who made the eyes but I?' "

OPEN LETTER FROM A CONSTANT READER

To all who carve their love on a picnic table
or scratch it on smoked glass panes of a public toilet,
I send my thanks for each plain and perfect fable
of how the three pains of the body, surfeit,

hunger, and chill (or loneliness), create
a furniture and art of their own easing.
And I bless two public sites and, like Yeats,
two private sites where the body receives its blessing.

Nothing is banal or lowly that tells us how well
the world, whose highways proffer table and toilet
as signs and occasions of comfort for belly and bowel,
can comfort the heart too, somewhere in secret.

Where so much constant news of good has been put,
both fleeting and lasting lines compel belief.
Not by talent or riches or beauty, but
by the world's grace, people have found relief

from the worst pain of the body, loneliness,
and say so with a simple heart as they sit
being relieved of one of the others. I bless
all knowledge of love, all ways of publishing it.

THE MISER

I was out last night,
the very picture of a sneak, dark and hunched-over,
breaking and entering again.
Why do I do it?

And why, when I can afford serious residences,
do I keep to this one room?
Perhaps if I had not lost track of the difference
between the real and the ideal
it would never have happened.
I hide here almost entirely now.

When I go out, when I creep into those silent houses,
I steal newspapers.
An armload, no more than I can carry comfortably.
Sometimes they are already tied up
on the side porch or by the kitchen stove.
Nobody misses them.
They think each other or the maid
has carried them out to the street.

They say there is something intractable out there,
the Law, the Right to Privacy,
the World.
In the days when my obsession was only a wound-up toy,
squeaking and jabbering in my chest,
I could have believed them.

I sit by the window today
(There is very little space left now,
though I have left corridors wide enough to walk through
so I won't lose touch)
holding my latest on my lap,
handling them, fondling them, taking in every column.
They are becoming more and more precious.

My delusion grows and spreads.
Lately it seems to me
as I read of murders, wars, bankruptcies, jackpot winnings,
the news is written in that perfect style
of someone speaking to the one
who knows and loves him.

Long before they miss me, I think,
the room will be perfectly solid.
When they break in the door and, unsurprised,
hardened to the most bizarre vagaries,
begin to carry out my treasure,
death's what they'll look for underneath it all,
those fluent, muscled, imaginative men,
sweating in their innocent coveralls.

But I will be out in broad daylight by then,
answering,
having accepted utterly the heart's conditions.
Tell them I wish them well, always,
that I've been happy.

COLORADO

Going up or coming down,
I'll give you an earful, the mountain said.
Going up, we stopped at nine thousand feet
under the pressure of that message.

Lake, cabin and stream
are enclosed by the tops of mountains.
The scenery is self-referring,
and here it is best to be provincial,
as in love or avarice.

Whose silly system
tries, every day or two, to scramble higher
toward a bearcave or abandoned mine
in order to look into the mountain?
Mine, pumping and slipping
where pungent rabbitbrush
thrusts up its pubic bush all over
the slope, and Cottonwood Creek
spurts from up there,
its trout hidden as sperm.
Back down in the cabin my bossy heart
tells me for hours how hard it is
to speed up the whole business.

"Rhythmic alternation . . . rocks and lulls attention like the
beating of a silver hammer on metal"

They have taken the silver, those early lovers,
and gone; the half-hour sex hotels
in Leadville, St. Elmo and Buena Vista
are closed. Now, to take in this country,
I must close my eyes, loosen my hold on the pen,
take off my clothes and fall.
One simple agony
and there I'd be, the stream
between my spraddled legs,

foxtail grasses stroking each nerve-end
the whole wild length of my body, hair
tangled in penstemon, buckwheat flower
and tansy aster, chest
pierced by a stand of quaking aspen
straight through the heart, *tremuloides* too.
I'd never get up.

". . . a ghost town of Colorado Mining heyday, it is stirring to
life as a tourist center high in the Rockies"

But look, still humpbacked with slag, the crone
can feel seemly once more, forget and forgive.
Under an ancient, many-turreted hat,
her fresh fluorescent face—
lifted by Sportswear, Sportinggoods
and J. C. Penney—burns,
and her heart is gushing silver again.
Anyone can see. A shameless sign
says "This Way To The Trout Hatchery."

Oh, no one's so innocent this time.
It's possible still, with camper and rod,
to snag out silver and go—
but only so much silver, for a foreknown fee.
What's possible again is some
sophisticated mutual exploitation.

"Affection . . . strikes one with a silence like that of Adam before
he had even named the beasts"

At the end of each slow, ascending S,
we seize from Cottonwood Pass,
each time a bit diminished, the same sight,
an exercise in both return
and aspiration.

Colorado

Twelve thousand feet high, at the top,
there's a small gravelled pull-off, and
(oh yes, we can bring
our bodies along this far)
a tiny toilet of peeled pine.
We stand still, mortal and improbable.
The world is all below us, we can choose
whether to go back down on one side
of the mountain, or the other.

Holding above us a strange snow
that stays for lifetime after lifetime,
the tips of mountains seem like merest hills.
One can almost forget
the wind, the ropes, the cold, the crampons,
avalanches, weaknesses of heart,
but still we only look,
hoping at best to learn a little from the view.
I'll go back down to be
the tourist that I am, and I suppose
that you will too.

"Regular return has . . . the sleep-inducing effect of monotony
. . . poetic ordering has reduced affective pressure"

If I hauled to the top of the hill
my private enterprise,
and, bent to suds of cloud,
washed once and for all
from my lips and eyes
the sexual grimace,
I wouldn't be afraid
to open a silver claim
and try digging with skill
where recurrence has no place,

"The tendency to sleep qualifies, softens . . . so that we are
assaulted from a tolerable distance or through a protective screen"

but before that climb,
since I'm so heavily here,
turn away from my face,
my dear and more dear,
and the whore's face of Time.
Rest, and believe
this metrical disgrace:
your heart has kept its silver
and all silver strikes recur.
Sleep, love.
For you I made this rhyme.

WHAT I WANT TO SAY

I

It is as simple as it can be.
I will leave off my clothes
(which is a kind of leveling, isn't it?)
and address you as nakedly
as anyone can.

Each one is perfect,
that is what I want to say.

There is no one perfection,
only an exercise of loving.
And it is always extraordinary.
One wild iris clump,
carried from Maine in a coffee can,
this third year gave me, in the mild summer,
twenty-one exquisite blue flowers.
A showy ten, then a more delicate seven,
then, further down on the stems,
an unlooked-for four.

"Tukaram . . ."
(I am telling you as nakedly as I can)
It happens in time.

When, somewhere, one wave of the sea begins moving,
one moved by the sun, let us say,
the next by the stars, let us say,
the next by the moon,
(I told you you would never believe it)
it is not spent.
It folds back and reenters the sea,
where it is indistinguishable from any other,
the sea who says each time,
"It is what I am."

I I
What do you think love is, anyway?
I'll tell you, a harrowing.
And I stand here helpless with what I know,
because in that Ministry
to be understood leads straight to the room
where understanding stops
and a final scream is that of the self
preserving itself.

To say I love you is a humiliation.
The weak tears gathering in the eyes
drip on a chessboard one fiddles with alone then,
mourning the betrayal of
some other possibility.
It is the absolute narrowing of possibilities,
and everyone, down to the last man,
dreads it.

I I I
It is the eye that calls, as if it were sleepless,
that says in its call, "Come to the window, see,
up there on some moonstruck table-land
a record is turning."

The eye calls the flesh from a sarabande
it is busy composing, "Come, there is something . . .
and not because it is there, because it is not yet there,
and who knows if it is complex, or simple.

That music neither of us can hear,
not transformations but changes,
will move us yet."

THE GOOD MAN

I

It is almost unbearably harmonious—
the purple petunias and stalks of lavender
with a blue couch pillow behind them.
The pillow fastens itself to the flowers
as if there were no space between but blue.
Let beauty fill in spaces where there is no good man.
But if there is a good man, let him put his head
on the blue pillow, and his yellowish face
will interfere with the flowers, and the natural
will become, in an instant, historical, and the historical
will become, in a little while, dramatic.

II

"A kind of unskillful desire to give life more thickness." GIDE

The dog chews up rye bread and spits it out.
He will do it ten times. It is his humanity.

On the stained and whiskery skin of the world
we walk, bumping shins and knees on things,
but live in our heads, in the sugar and gall
of language, bumping our heads on each other.
If a bird flies down from a tree and lights
on his finger, the good man is surprised.
That is not his forte. He moves words,
and his knees and elbows move to the meaning
of words, through the high stubble of things.

III

"How do you *know* a fish doesn't suffer
as much as you do?" the biochemist asked
with anguish. But he was not the good man.
And I too am sickened sometimes by the heaviness
of things to be done. Little roadbuilders, like ants,

swarming to carry away a mountain.
Taking care of a house—to reach the top,
to lift and wash its parts and partitions.
On rainy days my hair gains weight
as if somebody's tears hung in the follicles,
somebody treated unjustly, unthinkingly,
somebody called by the wrong name.
For the good man, to move a mountain one grain
of dust at a time is to move a mountain.
For him the act is laid in the idea
like honey in a honeycomb. We are here for that.
He eats honey without compunction.

THE CHALLENGER

Old liar, death, do you think I don't see you?
There is not one of your masks I don't know,
even this one, soft and winning—the half-truth.

When the fruit in its bowl turns green I see you, death.
When a sleep-walker hears the clock hands unwind,
when a hand jerks back from a reaching hand.

Even in the motion of rest I touch your face.
I know its shape in love, and in the wit of madness.
I will face up to you, my sleepy lover.

I will fight you with nuance and with clearness,
with the making and breaking of form and measure,
with a greedy face and with an immaculate.

I will lie with clocks, which are always a little late,
I will lie with madness, with the fact that you love me,
and for a long time you will believe me.

RELATIONSHIPS

The legal children of a literary man
remember his ugly words to their mother.
He made them keep quiet and kissed them later.
He made them stop fighting and finish their supper.
His stink in the bathroom sickened their noses.
He left them with sitters in lonesome houses.
He mounted their mother and made them wear braces.
He fattened on fame and raised them thin.

But the secret sons of the same man
spring up like weeds from the seed of his word.
They eat from his hand and it is not hard.
They unravel his sweater and swing from his beard.
They smell in their sleep his ferns and roses.
They hunt the fox on his giant horses.
They slap their mother, repeating his phrases,
and swell in his sight and suck him thin.

TO POETS' WORKSHEETS IN THE
AIR-CONDITIONED VAULT OF A LIBRARY

I
Shall we assume that the world
is waiting to hear how this speech happened,
pretending to be busy about other things,
a housewife on the verge of an affair,
tending the bomb,
clipping in the ruffled borders,
her face rapt and serious, almost saintly,
her poor tempted eyes always looking the other way?
Who can say what the world wants, or waits for?
The only thing we know is so simple
we hardly dare say it.
People keep trying to speak to each other.

I I
We are all fools, anyway, of one kind or another,
down on one knee to the imagination,
too scared to do much, in that ridiculous posture,
but hope she didn't hear a creak of the old bones.
Or else convinced she is leaning over our deathbed
while we, like Ralph, whisper our touching and absurd
goodbye: "If you've been hated you've also been loved.
Ah but, dear Lady, *adored!*"
When all the long love-lorn while
the problem was one of believing our own recognitions,
no doubt the greatest foolishness of all.
May one note here, nevertheless, that to believe them
is occasionally useful?

I I I
Without turning the light on,
somebody snatched five words from a nightmare
in the scrawl of a blind Titan.
Up the Christmas list,

past the black currant jelly and over the electric sander,
a little judgment meanders.
Trying to say it, trying to say,
the typewriter sputters its clogged e
into a big printed HAPY BIRTHDAY DADDY.
A minnow flipped out of the eye's pond
into this bar napkin
which keeps it moistened.
Twenty Xed-out lines and "Oh hell with it. Oh shit."
The slapped mouth reddens
on a yellow second-sheet.

IV

I woke last night
to see these leaves falling through the air,
and in its labor,
letting its leaves fall, yellow and white,
the mind standing like a tree,
suffering its changes.
And I seemed to hear in a half-sleep
something feeding and pressing up
from the ground where this waste fell,
something fruited and gentle.

V

That body gracing the sofa with such a studied sprawl,
smoking a cigarette to kill the taste of the last
heart-of-artichoke marinated in a court bouillon,
two fingers twitching at its imported, unfamiliar,
badly tied ascot
and talking about Malcolm Muggeridge—
who could guess that this very moment in its heart-of-hearts
it wants to be halfway across the country
kissing the eyelids of someone it's never been introduced to,
saying, "You interest me strangely."
Saying, "Nobody has ever listened to me like this before."

V I

Stay, then, in that cool place.
The world itself creates
possibility after possibility,
constantly erupts, and quiets.

When shape and shapeliness come together
in a quiet ceremony of chance,
page after page will finally be delivered
into the perfect hands.

THE TWINS

My sweet-faced, tattle-tale brother was born blind,
but the colors drip in his head. He paints with his fingers.
All day with his pots and paper he follows me around
wherever I set up my easel, till I pinch his bat ears,

then before he goes he swears he didn't feel anything.
But he knows my feelings, sneaks them out of my skin.
The things he knows! Leaving me squeezed and sulking,
he pretends he felt them himself and tells everyone.

Nobody ever blames him. He's terribly talented.
The world, glimpsing itself through him, will grow
sick with self-love, it seems, and under his eyelid
lie down, in burning shame, with its own shadow,

whereas, on my canvas, it wears its gray and brown
like a fat beaver, and even as I sweat on my brush,
all forms, at its simple-minded toothy grin,
branches, limbs, trunks, topple in a watery backwash.

When he goes to sleep, he says, the world stays in his head
like a big spiderweb strung between ear and ear,
buzzing like telephone wires, and what he has heard
all night, next morning has happened, is true, is there.

Though it always comes back for me, thick, bathed, grateful,
everything has to be re-imagined each sunrise
when I crawl from my black comfort. But I can't make a phone
   call.
I have to talk to something in front of my eyes.

You'd never know we were close. When we meet strangers
they poke my round stomach and pat his long bare legs,
I gush, and he, or that's what it looks like, glares,
then he stomps on my oils and we fight like cats and dogs.

The Twins

But when it rains sometimes, and he feels it and I hear it,
and he closes my eyes with his fingers to stop my raining,
and one tear falls before everything is quiet,
and his tear is the color of cinnamon on my tongue,

oh then we leave together and nobody can find us.
Not even our mother, if she came, could tell us apart.
Only the stars can see, who cluster around us,
my painted person crouched in his painted heart.

LEDA RECONSIDERED

She had a little time to think
as he stepped out of water
that paled from the loss of his whiteness
and came toward her.
A certain wit in the way he
handled his webbed feet,
the modesty of the light that lay on him,
a perfectly clear, and unforgiveable,
irony in the cock of his head
told her more than he knew.
She sat there in the sunshine,
naked as a new-hatched bird,
watching him come,
trying to put herself
in the place of the cob, and see
what he saw:

flesh comfortable, used,
but still neatly following the bones,
a posture relaxed,
almost unseemly, expressing
(for the imagination,
unlike the poor body it strips and stirs,
is never assaulted)
openness, complicity even,
the look of a woman
with a context in which she can put
what comes next
(no chance of maiden's hysteria
if his beak pinched hold of her neck-skin,
yet the strangeness of the thing
could still startle her
into new gestures,)
and something—a heaviness,
as if she could bear things,

or as if, when he fertilized her,
he were seeding the bank she sat on,
the earth in its aspect of
quiescence.

And now, how much would she try
to see, to take,
of what was not hers, of what
was not going to be offered?
There was that old story
of matching him change for change,
pursuing, and at the solstice
devouring him.
A man's story.
No, she was not that hungry
for experience. She had her loves.
To re-imagine her life—
as if the effort were muscular
she lifted herself a little
and felt the pull at neck
and shoulderblade, back
to the usual.
And suppose she reached with practiced arms
past the bird, short of the god,
for a vulnerable mid-point,
and held on,
just how short-sighted would that
be? Would the heavens in a flurry record
a major injustice to the world's
possibilities?

He took his time,
pausing to shake out a wing.
The arrogance of that gesture!
And yet she saw him
as the true god.

She saw, with mortal eyes
that stung at the sight,
the pain of his transformations,
which, beautiful or comic,
came to the world
with the risk of the whole self.
She saw what he had to work through
as he took, over and over,
the risk of love,
the risk of being held,
and saw to the bare heart
of his soaring, his journeying,
his wish for the world
whose arms he could enter in the image
of what is brave or golden.

To love with the whole imagination—
she had never tried.
Was there a form for that?
Deep, in her inmost, grubby
female center
(how could he know that,
in his airiness?)
lay the joy of being used,
and its heavy peace, perhaps,
would keep her down.
To give: women and gods
are alike in enjoying that ceremony,
find its smoke filling and sweet.
But to give up was an offering
only she could savor,
simply by covering
her eyes.

He was close to some uncommitted
part of her.
Her thoughts dissolved and
fell out of her body like dew
onto the grass of the bank,
the small wild flowers,
as his shadow,
the first chill of his ghostliness,
fell on her skin.
She waited for him so quietly that
he came on her quietly,
almost with tenderness,
not treading her.
Her hand moved into the dense plumes
on his breast to touch
the utter stranger.

THE VOYEUR

The sizzle of the Coleman
seals off fir, birch and underbrush
with their mixed bag of onlookers who
scuffle at the edge, held back
by light from claiming garbage
and clearing as wild favors,
and detaches both the path to the lake,
crossed sometimes by deer or partridge
in lunatic self-absorption,
and its continuance,
a chill path the moon
laid down over the heads of simple-minded
swimmers, from the cabin's
hot work of being human.
Pants and bra dangle
from one hand. On the kitchen wall
behind her the machines of her usefulness,
washed and hung up, take on a glittery, ornamental life,
the book, in a gnat-specked circle
of white brilliance, is closed,
the vacant half of a bed
beside her, open. She faces
the window, wondering
what encroachments, if any,
will take place this night.

Like the pinch of a deerfly
she feels flank, then throat
lit on, focussed on,
and, shading her eyes at the glass,
makes out, mid-path, something big that the moon
is back of, neither the stilted poise
of a deer, nor a bear's upright,
goofy and amiable-looking
assessment of darkness,

but something the night wizens,
something hunched.
And so she believes its gaze
belongs to her, that its feeding
is abstract enough to overlook
the clearing's juicy tufts,
bitten flesh and bones in the garbage,
and fall on hers. Matchmaker
for the ark of this moment,
she selects a shape
out of the great plenty of the woods
to get along with.

She straightens, but stays,
and lowers her eyes, lest their looks,
hers and the other's,
lock and fall down together, wrestling
in the shrubby borderline between them,
suddenly feeling herself
so showy, so lighted,
she wants his eyes to find the
pure recipience she has turned to
and bring it . . . what? Anything,
sweet, sacred, or evil,
in his attention.
Slowly, arms over head,
she begins to enter a new dress,
her nakedness, steam-fitted
by his eye to each slope and point.
She is entering it
with the whole imagination cor tracted
to him, to what he sees,
and as her breasts swell and press
on cups of a fabric unfashionably
sleek, as belly, thighs,
wrists, ankles are being contained
in his donation,

she believes if he winked
out there in the moonlight
one side of her would go numb.

The gassy, effusive lamp
holds its breath until
she has been wholly seen,
until this first act of creation's
perfect little comedy is over.
When it throws against the wall
her humpy twin of dark dough,
handled for twenty years,
she has shed their kinship,
she has shed belief
that the strongest love is habitual.
As at dusk on the beach
a sandal slipping squeezes out
from between rocks a green air,
so she feels herself flavored.
A tongue, touched between neck and shoulder
would find the wild mint.

Feeling too clear,
she hides behind her arms
and leans to the window.
He slinks into the black clutter
beside the path.
Given her form and left to find
its function, she'd like to see him now,
rock at the bait of her breast
his cheek, whose stubble
would snag the fresh silk,
wipe his wet mouth with her lips,

return under his grip
to creased, to rumpled
thing that manhood mounts,
go into the woods even
to claim an animal who couldn't
believe his eyes.

ALONG THE ROAD

The ticker tapes roll down my sides
with the same quotation: midsummer;
field green, pine green; market steady.
For three days I have taken on faith
continuous, complicated negotiations
of the pricked-eared, calculating-eyed
under, let us say, ferns, cattails,
and profitable buzz in, surely, fieldflowers,
clover, as I take on faith
on the longest expressway
the courting embraces of father and mother,
congressional pity, presidential wisdom,
the entrance of bullets into real flesh,
over and over, the end of my life.
But now one ribbon breaks for a flaming
moment, cheek, shoulder, rib, hip
turn hot. Wait. Onto the green,
glazed retina comes
an explosion of hurled orange.
They are burning the dump.
Even in the afterthoughts, black, gray,
seeping through the sky like rivers
feeling out new beds, damping down
tops of trees and a steeple, threatening
to inundate a hillful of little houses
in pebble colors, the eye turns
back where something was seen.
Stay there with me, my dear,
free from the reticence
of ordinary incineration, and watch.
During the first days there will be
only an interruption, gorgeous, mutual,
of the texture and temperature of the world,
a representation by three of its acres
of uproar, extravagance, primitivism, seething,

and our senses will tire from it
as they tire from any other
overmastering abundance, yet
we will use memory and imagination
to inform ourselves that it is a process
of reduction. In its center
something serious is happening.
This is what I want you to wait for.
When the flames lower themselves onto
their fearful bed, draw in on themselves,
devote themselves with unbelievable intensity
to this consummation, it is important
that your eyes and my eyes be wide open,
unchilled, immodest, focussed outward.
On the edge—we notice it together—the first
disclosure. Its spasms of hot white breath
stop. It is innocent of color,
and so without insinuation,
without suppliance. Black. Formal. Wry.
Black spirals spray up
over a black hummock and bent black bars
jam the entrances to black caverns,
while the mind runs backward for a last
reconstruction: springs and bones
have been bitten from their fat,
barrels, cans, cars
set free from the need to contain.
All over the area there goes on
a slow, entranced emergence
of things out of the ashes of their usefulness.
There is nothing seasonal here.
If we have lost sight of comfort,
of fleshy, vegetable consolations,
still we have arrived at an entanglement
of true weight, a landscape of certainties.

(Will you smile with me at one corner
where the lamp cranes its neck like an outraged hen
hearing indecencies from an egg
of a kettle beside it? The comic keeps.)
Let us make sure now
that no amount of imagining
could have furnished us with the particular
fusion over there, this antic
tin stretch, that petrified
moment of rage when something tried
to ooze out of its own nature,
eyeful by eyeful the exact, extensive
derangement. When you turn away, remember
none of this needs to be taken on faith;
it was all there when we were both looking.
Now let us go, each to his own
assumptions. Out of long habit
I myself will continue to suppose
that the planet can see out of either eye,
can subsidize its creatures with dark
as well as with light (though only
by squeak, snap and hoot have I ever envisioned
the night life of the woods)
and when it rolls
(I suppose, don't you, that it rolls?)
it may even be able to feel, bearing down
on its side, the contribution we've just
witnessed, our heavy,
drossless, dark deposit.
And though I turn and take stock again
in its indefinite green, out of long habit
I will continue to say
we were dealing back there at the dump with the planet's
shapeliest, least abstract business.

IV

"*From perfect Grief there need not be Wisdom or even memory.*"

MARRIAGE, WITH BEASTS

for Jarvis

Bringing our love to the zoo to see what species
it is, I carry my head under my arm,
you cradle yours; we will hold them up to cages
or set them back on perch at the proper moments.
Each inch of my skin tingles, and I guess
yours tingles, as in high fever or sex heat
it is also reminded of its old bestial uses,
for what happens here is as informal
as disease, and we, like lust, are serious
about making sense of a strange, entire surface.

We consider first a herd of some big bruisers
who toddle around in tap-shoes, musing, grazing,
slim of hip and giant at head and shoulders
like football players ready to butt or shove.
As unselfconsciously as trees drip mosses
they dangle tatters of their worn-out winter coats
and neither marry nor burn, being as couplers
wholly impersonal. "Intraspecific aggression"
is simply not in them. Clearer than we suppose
our lowered heads can speak, they speak: Lorenz.
A murderous rage is the force that through green fuses
drives the daisies of love. Why yes, sweet mate,
your face and dress are dearer than anyone else's.
Why yes, life's light, we could kill each other with pillows.

Then come, my Moor in embryo, and let us
look at the birds and tease our remarkable hearts
with flocks of bright little resemblances.
Behind the glass they fly as if they were free,
and flash like multi-colored fingernails
of fingers that reach to all the keys of the air
and sound them for us. Holding such weight in our headbowls,
such stuffing, not of straw, but metaphors,
how can we scoop up these endless symphonies?

Lifted to birds, my scoop at least reminds you
to see through the great discrepancy of size
and find our own disorder, a birds-eye view.
My dear, your head heavily says, though earth
receives as "a tiny burden" a bird's death,
the burden swells, for one other bird, to despair
the size of the world. My dearest, mine replies,
the size of the world, sun, moon and stars
for the little while that he waits alone in bare
ruins of the choir where last she sang
and trills, but much too late, Oh stay, thou art fair.

At the pond we put on our heads, for the fowl here
will make us feel at home for a moment, being
the big-boned and aetherial mixed together.
Under such wings Leda conceived, and in
her lap "erst empfand er glücklich sein Gefieder."
The flamingo, testing each of his distant footsteps,
looks like the Duc de Guermantes, who trembles and teeters
on the high stilts of his eighty or more years.
Think how we've raised our own eyes from the ground
and tell me if we must tuck our heads in a wing,
my chilling redbreast, or watch the swans mount air
and take from their gyres terror or comforting.

At a farther pond we're going past, a "wallow
of flesh" lifts up its simple putty face. "Blou-
augh!" it says to me. Does it say that to you?

Shall we stop and find out if the monkeys wink too much?
As at Charenton, we hear these fools gibber,
and my head, that watches the "watched spectator" see
them throwing dung and garbage at one another,
grins, then ducks back in the lair of my arms
as your eyes pelt it with revulsion and pity.

Headstrong now, we enter the Nursery door
with a crowd of parents and children. My famished lover,
see how the tiger kit lays back his ears
for the bliss of his bottle. See, inside the oven
of the incubator, each wolf like a new-baked bun.
What can I feed you but old love over again?
That monkey mite, you say, I was thinking, rather,
how he hung like a rare sweet medal on his mother
as she swung up to the bars in a line by Swenson.
Tell me, my own perverse heroine,
making a public display of how bare you are,
what necklace of love can I ever bring you to wear?
The cubs box, but we stop their show. On either
side of the glass the charming babies stare
and whimper to see two grown-ups rocking each other.

In the raw, menstrual smell of the lion house
we go for a last stroll. Nemerov sparrows
make free with kings, being willing to eat their shit.
As far distant as they can get from the hose
that flushes away bones, flies and urine,
snooting the praise of their dumpy audience,
the cats stride with the strained hauteur of fashion
models, back and forth, rippling their coats.
We're tired of disguises, but what else can we look at?
Wait. A mountain lion stops and gazes
at me. He comes straight at me up to the bars
and stays there, looking me in the eye. He neither
implores nor threatens, he is only after some sight.
I see the slit in his iris. I think of Jeffers'
obsessed will to arrive at the inhuman
view, of Dickey, who began to act out his own
animal when he caught the eye of a panther.
A lightening whirl, snarl, rake at her face
with his spiked paw, and the lion discounts his mate,
coming up to see. She leaves. He sees me alone.

But I've lost my head, it rolls on the floor in spit
and candy wrappers, spilling. I get it back on.
Something, through his eye-slit, irradiates
my bones to simmering heat. In stillness. What is it?
No god is there. I feel nothing Ledean.
What can it be that comes without images?
An eye, nothing in it but what he is,
the word, then,

after all this,

not love but

LION?
The slit widens. There. Illiterate.
Perfect. lion. without adjective.
lion lionlionlion   it ceases
to be a word

    but I get away, turning to where you are.
I'm shaking. Now take what you've seen of me home, and let's
go on with our heady life. And treat me, my pet,
forever after as what I seem; for it seems,
and it is, impossible for me to receive,
under the cagey wedlock of your eyes,
what I make it impossible for you to give.

BEDTIME STORIES
1972

BEDTIME STORIES

So early into a big bed stowed out of sight,
child that I was, wide awake from the day, the day
of chiding and loneliness, unspent energy
in muscle and bone, ("growing pains"), the day's light
still promising from the window, would toss and yell,
"Grandma, Grandma! Please come and sit by me.
Tell me a story! Tell me another story!"
All that was missed, radio, books, pre-school,
hours of TV, music, long good-nights said,
the thrilling, calling, right-after-supper play
of the other kids in their far-off pom-pom-pullaway,
would come in the voice of an old woman by the bed.

ONE

An old widow lady, and went out to do her chore,
and had a cow, a few little things,
a few chickens, she was on the farm.
And went out to feed them and milk and gether
the eggs and thought she'd go in now, it was late, and get supper.
It was kinda late, she'd monkeyed around some more.

And she washed her few dishes and set down to read.
Lit the lamp and set down to read.
Well, and while she was readin happened to look
into the bedroom, just had two rooms—
one kinda bedroom, a room to eat, what she had—
and happened to see it, a man under there, the bed.
His feet, she seen his feet.

And she looked real close and seen it, a man layin there.
And never one word, but walked around and got
her Bible and she read, and she read real loud,
I forgot what chapter, that I can't tell you any more.
And then she prayed, I can tell you, prayed it all loud,
the Lord to save her and all like that, you know.
And went in and undressed for bed with the man still there.
And kneeled in front of the bed yet and prayed
when she had her clothes all off, she prayed the Lord.

Well then she laid down, laid kinda breathin hard
but she wasn't sleep. And well then the fella that heard
crawled out from under the bed and he sneaked
just like a whipped dog and never done
one thing, out of the house, and she went to sleep.
And she slept, that was all she said she did.
That's just what she said.
And I was too young to remember her name, just a kid.

And that man sneaked off and never harmed one
thing in the house. And that's true.
This lady I stayed with, I had to herd cattle, *Ja*, so,
we was all alone one night and she told me that
and that's all true, *Kleine*, all true.

TWO

After midnight, and my sister Lizzie
got awful sick and got the doctor and she thought,
though, she hadda die.
She kept saying she'd hafta die.
So Mother says to me and Sophie we
should go to Richsmeier my uncle, a mile to go.
Run cross the fields and it was pitch dark and rain.
And as we run long the road there was cornfield,
and we had hold of each other's hand yet
and run just as tight as we could run.

And all at once there was just like a great big black thing,
like a horse, only, oh, just like an elephant purt' near,
so big it was.
It made such a noise.
Oh just like a whirlwind, just a *whzzzzzzzzrrrrrr*
it was, how corn rattles, and, scare?
It scared us purt' near to death. It was dark out, but that
was still darker when it come out of there.
When it got there it come right out
of the cornfield and stood like it was growed there.

And it scared us purt' near to death, but we had
only four blocks like and then we was at my uncle.
Sophie just screamed and let go my hand and run,
and we run both of us like the dickens. Well then
we gave the door at Richsmeier's a shove,
the basket of corncobs in front the door and the broom
so the wind wouldn't blow it open I tell you we shoved
so they flew in the middle of the room.

Then we hollered, "Uncle, Uncle, get up quick."
And they got up and left us into the house
and we told them to hurry up, Lizzie was so sick
she said she hadda die. And they went with us

and when we got on the same place
Sophie just hollered and screamed like everything
but she just imagined it was still there. Uncle says,
"Don't holler. Now we're along with you." Then later
we got home and they stayed all night
and Lizzie got better.

My gosh, girl, that I seen with my own eyes.
It was the funniest thing like that I ever did see,
too. You'd never want to see one of those!

THREE

Such things there are, we don't know.
It makes a persond think all the time.
I can tell you one thing, though.

My mother's friend she lived in town, they told it,
it was in town yet,
that every night there come alwus such a big black cat
and walked "m'ow, m'ow" all round the house
when it come midnight.

And right next door was an old widow woman
wouldn't talk to nobody or nothin, but they never ketched
her doin nothin. They let her alone.

And every night the black cat would come "m'ow, m'ow".

And the friend my mother thought one day how she'd fix him
and she kept the washwater boilin
and at night when a black cat come, never come in the daytime,
sneaked her a kittle of water and leaned out the window
and throwed out washwater on it in the Lord's name.
And it *screamed*, screamed like I don't know what then,
yowled terrible loud, they could hear it in Heaven
almost. Oh I don't know,
I tell you it makes the shivers to come—
the next day the old widow woman
come out her house all humped up, and you know what?
She was scald on her face, her head,
right where the washwater flew.
And she never any more come in the cat.

I tell you,
I never forgot that.

Oh they told it alwus us kids, we shouldn't tease,
the Devil might be there because
that old widow woman was really scald.
Oh *Kind*, there is more in this old world
than a persond knows.

FOUR

Oh well, they had such a big garden
about half a block purt' near, and on two side
was all currants, planted in currant bushes
and one row was yet planted in the middle—that is,
one row currants, and one row gooseberries.
One row gooseberries on the other side.
And then four rows of great big tame grapes
through the other side, the south side of the garden.
Do you think us kids could pick a bunch of grapes?
The folks thought they could sell 'em but they wouldn't get
to town in time and they'd all rot.
Sometimes Father would go out and cut us
a bunch or so, but us kids wouldn't dare to pick.
Them grapes all went to waste, peck after peck,
Father never bought no sugar.
Only thing they did do was make this sorghum molasses.
That I ate on our bread all year.

To school, when we was at school, we had white lard
and a little salt sprinkled over on our bread,
and that was what we eat at school.
Nowadays if folks can't have two, three thick on their bread
they go on relief and the govment spreads it all.

But believe me when the cherries was ripe,
then we had our time.
They was just by the bushel and bushel
and bushel. And the plums, by jinks, then we had our fill.
Apples we didn't have many, Father plant that,
a big orchard, but they wasn't bearin yet.

FIVE

That was in 1875, then we moved here
with five covered wagons and we had seven cows with us.
And then we'd have to walk by spells, we'd change off
and one would drive the cows and then the other
one would. We sure seen some tough
times, sometimes people would be nice
and sometimes they wouldn't. We had to sleep in three of
the covered wagons, and sometimes, I tell you
it rained and dripped on our face.

We was on the road nine days.

One time we had a sick horse, and then
we stopped because it wouldn't walk any more.
We stopped by a horse doctor, and when
he got the medicine ready and start to give it
the horse, it dropped down dead, the horse.
Then a big thunder shower came up and they had
to bury it in the rain, such rain
that the water came right through the house.
I laid on the floor and just got soaked.

You see, we went over the Mississippi river
with a steamboat from Savannah Illinois to Sebulah
Iowa. When we stopped at Savannah
we stopped at a stone quarry, great big high
one, maybe one hundred fifty feet high.
Then one of the men with us stepped to the hill
at the edge and looked, how deep it was, and the whole
thing gave way with him. A great big oak yet,
right at the back of him, and these limbs was hangin
down where he was. He just grabbed one
and saved from fallin one hundred fifty feet.

Sometimes, them old wolves would howl
so at night, and gee,
then I couldn't sleep at all.

One time we stopped at a town and was gonna buy
some feed for the horses, they wouldn't let us have it.
They wanted us to stay there all night
and land knows what they was goin to do with us.
And Uncle said we wouldn't stay, they wouldn't let
us buy the feed. We drove on couple miles further,
it was all wild timber and it got kind of late.
When we got through all the wild timber
we come to a nice great big farm place. We stopped there
and asked could we stay all night, and, oh, they sure
wanted us to stay there.
They opened the gate for us and started a fire
and we got our supper.
And then the whole family come out and one of the men
that was along with us could play the accordion
and sing so nice, and they listened to that.
We set up till midnight.

SIX

That was in 1875, and we come through
another big timber and come to a farmhouse
that had lot of grapes. But they was a ways
from the house and two men that was with us
tried to snipe some and they got ketched.
The people act mean at first but they was good
after all, and let 'em have some like folks should.

The next day or so, I and my uncle had to drive
the cows, the covered wagons quite a ways ahead.
They come past one place there was a lot of tatoes
growin. Them two young men was so hungry and thought they'd
stop and dig some, we wouldn't have to buy
for supper. But then the man that owned the tatoes
ketched them. When Uncle and I
got there with the cows, that fellow was lookin at his tatoes
yet. He wanted to know if we were that outfit gone on
with the mover wagons, and we told him yes.
He told my uncle he'd ketched them two boys
was stealin his tatoes and he was gonna stop us
at the next town and settle with us but he never
showed up and we never seen him again.

I was just a kid, youngest of the three girls,
and we all had to sleep in the wagon box—the wagon
box, it was, it sure was no wider than
forty inch. And them other two big girls
got me in the middle and purt' near killed me off.
They slept all night and I couldn't rest, they was bother
me, so big and I just a kid. So I got
me a couple box in back of the wagon, off
from them, and that's where I slept on top.
I got me a blanket and I slept on top there.
I tell you, I had to sleep somewhere.

Then we didn't have no more trouble and we
had a lot of fun too, and we got to Ackley.

Well, that was Saturday, day before Easter.
You know Gust, he alwus said there
was no Easter Rabbit, that's what he said.
He alwus said it was us that did it, colored
them eggs. Well so then one day it was the day
before Easter, they hadda plant tatoes so Mother
took the two kids along in the fields, she helped
plant tatoes that day. I didn't have to.

And while they was gone I got busy.
Sewed them eggs in the purtiest pieces from prints,
just made six or seven.
I had them purty pieces from Mrs. Ribberger
and I sewed them on.
Ja, and I got some wood ashes and filled my pan
and I packed my eggs in there and cover
'em up with the wood ashes. And then pour
boilin water over it, boiled 'em good and hard
about six or seven minutes, they was good and hard.

Then I took 'em out and put 'em in cold water
and after that I took the cloth off and oh
wasn't they purty! Honest, the purtiest I ever
seen, oh they was purty. And then when I had 'em
all done and laid 'em away, well then after supper
they monkeyed around a little bit and they got so
tired, went to bed. And those kids was gonna be sure
and shake the ashes out of the stove so they'd be sure
I didn't boil any so that there was no fire.
Thought I'd make 'em yet when they got to sleep.

Well and then they went to bed.
After they had that shook out they went to bed.
And you know, ennahow, they had their
nests made in the wardrobe or what they call that
and that big box below, kind of a drawer.

So when they was good upstairs why Father
made a big racket on the porch, and I had
all the eggs in their nests, laid 'em quick in their nests.
And Father made another big racket, that the Rabbit
went out again. Then Father called
'em down and they come head over heels downstair.
Ja, and then they looked in their nests and seen yet
them purty eggs. Then Gust and Anna alwus
went to Father, "Father, did the Easter Rabbit
lay them eggs?" "Yes." Then they'd run
alwus to Mother, "Mother, did the Easter Rabbit
lay them eggs? Did you see him?" "Yes."

Then Gust believed there was an Easter Rabbit,
cause nobody could color eggs like that.
That sure was fun.

EIGHT

Well, that old big fat man
he'd walk through Father's pasture to go see his friend,
goin there, and he'd stay a long time, and goin
back it would maybe be midnight.

They alwus said that the old pasture was spooked.
I never seen nothin, I looked,
and this fat guy didn't believe it either.
Well I been all over that old pasture
from one end to the other
as long as we lived there and I never seen
a ditch or noplace on there.

So that one night when he went his friend, why he got
in a ditch comin back. Then he worked and worked that the sweat
run off him and he couldn't get out.
And he swore, he just cussed one after the other.
And he tried and tried, Lord knows how long in there
he worked and couldn't get out.
Then when he couldn't get out he started prayin.
Ja, then he got out
cause there was no such a big ditch,
nobody could see how he got in such a big ditch,
and I knew this fellow good, a big fat man.

Then my father had sold that farm and the neighbors wrote
he should come and get his farm back it was spooked.
he should come take it back again.

Well I never seen nothin.

NINE

That was my grandfather, nearly went to prison.
I'm your grandmother and he was my grandfather, so
you must say. In the Old Country, and they was poor
and then if they could get to a big town some way,
why you see they could buy thing cheaper.
So he and another man, a friend of hisn
ennaway, I don't know who he was, they thought
they'd go to a bigger place and get stuff cheaper,
coffee and sugar and such thing like that.

And you see, they wouldn't dare to go to big place,
they'd get watched, some officer or police
would watch for them alwus. Because these poor people
in the little towns, why they would all run
to big towns to trade, and that they wouldn't dare
to do, had to stay in their own town.

So him and the fella, they went to them big towns,
go in the daytime and sneak back at night.
And so when they come back with a load, they had bought
a lot of stuff, they got caught in this timber.
The officer ketched them there.
Well and they start to run and he after them
and this brushwood was all piled in piles,
and it was so pitch dark they hid in the brush piles.
And they hid under them.

Then that fella, police, he come along with his spear,
he couldn't find 'em any other place,
so he come to the piles where my Grandfather
was in. And he stuck a spear in and the spear
just run whzzzz past his face.
Three, four times he stuck it in there
and the one time it just went past him.
The other fella didn't get it at all, that was with him.

Then you see they had to stick in there three,
four hours, the way he said, because the policeman
would stay there and watch first. And toward morning they
crawled out all right and safe. He saved his head.
They got their stuff all home too, he would say.
And then he would laugh, my grandfather.
"They didn't get me ennaways," he alwus said.
That's all there was in it, that's all I can remember.

TEN

In the Old Country, then, two ladies and two boys,
each had a boy, they alwus went the neighborhood,
ever place they'd go. Take a basket alwus, the two
old women, they'd be beggin all the time, they'd
maybe want somethin to eat or so.
And the two boys alwus run a block ahead
and them mothers alwus talk about people, what they say.

And some neighbor came to my grandmother's, well,
then they talked that it was a fright them two women
alwus go run around and beg from somebody else.
And this lady wished somebody'd scare them once
that they didn't know where to go.
So my father heard that that they wished somebody
would scare them once, and so
that night Father hunted his father's nightshirt
and he knew just which way them women hadda come,
and he put that nightshirt on.
And them kids come a block ahead purty soon.
And then when Father heard them he stood like that
with his arms up this way, all in white.

And the kids when they seen him got scared, they run back,
told their mothers that there was a spook,
a ghost or whatever standin in the road there.
And one mother said there was no such thing, no spook.
And they said they went so long in the Lord's name,
they was goin tonight, there was nobody hurtin them.

And they went up close, they wasn't fraid, they said,
and one woman got so close was gonna look
in his face, and it scared Father so
that he dropped his hands, his hands fell down.
And then they run, they screamed and run
and the apples and pears and plum
was all rolled out of the basket, they laid
all over the road.

Next day they come to my grandma, was tellin her oh
what a scare they had. That they run
and they lost all the apples and nuts what they had.
That there really was a spook, that he stood,
and was alive because his hands dropped down.
And they try and couldn't get Grandma to believe that.
Grandma said no, sure not. Oh, it was so!
And Father was up in the attic, he was spinnin wool,
and heard all that. And that's all.
They couldn't believe it but it was so.
After that they seen they got home in daytime.
That's a true story. Over a hundred years ago.

ELEVEN

Just full of springs the world was in Illinois
them days, and father had built a walk
from spring to spring. And snake?
There wasn't so many snake but they was these big
bull snake. I was gonna get the cows and there
was one, oh ennaway from here
to the wall, and Oh, I thought, and alwus spit
with the tongue. And Father was workin and saw what,
and was gonna jump on it but I held him back,
wouldn't let him. Well, because such a big fella I thought
it would bite him or sting, whatever they do.
Then he got such a big stick and knocked it senseless.
And it rolled in a ball, a bunch that big it was
before he knocked it senseless. And he had a club
and he killed it there. And he hung it
over a fence, the fence was so high
and both ends reached the ground. The kids all went
to look, such a big one they hadn't ever see.
In the middle it was just like my arm, so fat.
I can see it yet.

And such things, yet!
One of my sisters was baptized, I guess, and there come
company, and it got kinda late.
And way up in the corner of the pasture they had to walk,
my two older sisters—I was too young—had to milk
the two cows that give the most milk.
It was right in the summer time.
And somebody come all dressed in white, and it went
from cow to cow and looked under ever cow.
I didn't see it, just think of it now,
only the kids come runnin home and told it.
It was their cousind, you know, that's what they thought,
so they alwus kept talkin and it'd never say
a word and finally it come
so close to their cow and wouldn't talk, and when

it come so close they picked up their milk pails and run.
And they run and it come after them
and they come runnin home and all their milk spilt
and just scared to death.
They had just a cupful of milk in their pails
and they was tellin it, both.
Spilt all their milk, almost, so tight they run,
and never knew who it was that run
after them and it wouldn't talk or nothin,
that spook or thing or whatever.
Ach now, just think of it, that's how the world was then.
Things that you don't see no more.
There was something there.

TWELVE

Ja, we had it hard.
No butter, Father'd hafta sell it, on our bread.
No oley then, like they got now,
and we never got no bread sugared.
If the horse was sick, sometimes us kids pulled the plow
just like we was horses. And Mother, when she had the kids
us kids took care of the baby, Mother in the field.
We took turns to rock the baby, and if somebody come,
horsedoctor or so, we got scared and hid
behind the cradle, company hardly ever come.
Ja, they don't do that way no more.
They got things so good, go to the dimestore, grocerystore.
We'd piece quilts, purty pieces people give us,
pick chickens for our featherbeds, stuff 'em with feather.
So cold it was, but we musn't make no fuss.
When thunderstorms come, rain would come in on our face.
Such good roofing they have now, folks clean.
Why, *Kind*, every week when I got big enough
I'd comb out the girls' hair over the hot stove
and the lice would fall out and spit on the stove.

Sometimes we thought we'd sure hafta die.
Sometimes so sick we sure didn't know what to do.
Well, we made it ennahow.

THIRTEEN

We alwus had to herd cattle,
I and my brother, then we wouldn't dare
to come home at noon, Aunt Sophie was little
yet, she couldn't herd, just me and my brother.
Then we had to stay from morning to four,
then you see sometime we'd get hungry,
and right acrost the road there was a plum orchard,
you know they grow wild, where we had to herd.
It was all plums in a kind of a edge of a timber.
And about from here to the corner of main street there
was the owner of that land. And they had
such a darn smart dog, and they kinda mistrusted
we'd maybe go and steal plum.
And then this lady she'd send him up there, tell him—
I don't know his name—to go look and see
if the kids was under the plum tree.

And I was gonna get some plums one time,
you know they'd go all to waste enahow.
Well, and so we'd want some.
And she sent that dog, didn't want us to get 'em.
And you know when he seen me
he'd just walk on back to her
and when she asked him if we was there
he'd just kinda nod his head.

We knew that dog did that and when
we seen him I tell you we got out of there.
We didn't get no more plum.
He sure was the smartest dog I ever seen
in my life. Oh he was a smart devil.
I mean cuss, I said devil but I didn't mean.
That sounds awful.
If any hear that they think I was an awful one.
That sounds awful, like I don't know what.
I don't like for an old woman a word like that.

FOURTEEN

The folks built that barn, your great grandfather, and them
carpenters was alwus kinda lazy, didn't care
whether they done a day's work or not. *Ja,* Grandfather,
he grumbled about it one time, that they was fools,
they was just passin the time away sleepin.
You know and in the gangway of the barn then
they had a lot of hay and straw layin—
it was purt' near done—and there they'd alwus lay down
and sleep. So I and Fred we made up that we'd
fix 'em now oncet. And we had an old she-buck there,
she-buck-sheep there, you know he was a mean
old one, he'd buck us to beat the band.
He purt' near killed Fred, another time though,
and Fred was just a little fella.

So we got him good and mad, made out after he
was good and mad we run into the barn and then
one of us would run to one side and one
to the other. So he wouldn't buck us, buckin,
you see, he was mad. The carpenters was up
kinda high in the straw and he saw and when
he couldn't buck us he went after them fellows, and say
he give them the dickens on that straw . . .
And that scared them so I tell you their eye
stuck out so big me and Fred purt' near die
laughin and that old buck he kinda knibzulled 'em
and they was so sleep that they couldn't do nothin.

I tell you from that day on they never'd
lay in the gangway to sleep. He fixed 'em good.
Ach, just a kid, didn't think enahow that some day
I'd be tellin it all to my granddaughter yet.
Well, when they work they oughta work like they say.

Grandma, thank you for not making me earn.
I was born, that was enough for you, and I saw.
You came, enough for me, when I called Grandma.
No presents, no kisses, a little helpless concern.
When you died, only miracles let me forgive.
Simply by happening to each other, we blent.
Love unaided, both of us lived by that.
If artless love makes you live again, you live.

POEMS
1965–1973

THE FEAR OF FLYING

> ". . shall it be given us to speak in the spiritual,
> unearthly voice of a bat or a jet?"

At the airport, ready to leave on my little trip,
I tell you goodbye and start
to get in line at the door, our relationship
so old we don't kiss, when my heart

goes crazy with pain and fear, jumps in my throat,
my stomach heaves, I want
to get out of this frozen skin and run for the heat
of your body and yet I can't.

Every time I'm about to get on a plane it's the same
sick terror. I've got to know what
brings on such hysteria, what in God's name
is the matter with me. It's not

the fear of death. You've rehearsed me so often in that,
with your false springs, your icy
changes of heart and face, I'm bored at the thought
of there being no more me

to see and feel them. It's not as if we were young
and couldn't bear to part—
far from it. We've been yoked together so long
it doesn't even hurt

that we both forget every anniversary.
There were good years together,
one has to remember that toward the end, surely—
moondazzle, peach weather,

brilliant noons, eloquent storms, sweet
new spears of tenderness,
all the lovely things, natural and trite,
one has to believe, I guess,

make life worth living, made it worth our while
to have come to middle age
with such brutal knowledge of one another. How well
I know each clever image

you present in public, the four parts you play
(none of them now for me):
the cool, brittle, disillusioned roué,
handsome as a fall tree,

with secret softnesses beneath, to be found
and nursed into late bloom,
much rarer of course than of April's callow ground,
by someone in the room.

Or, your hair re-dyed, the hand-holder,
fresh buds in your buttonhole,
the whole green youth bit again, the breezy,
twittery, dancing, boy-girl

approach. (How you pull that bright illusion out
of the hat at your age
over and over, I'll never know. It's what,
watching it from offstage,

can hurt me most, whose one-and-only springtime
in one of yours is over.)
Or, with faintly snow-streaked hair, you mime
the quiet, fatherly lover,

all passion spent, not at all dangerous—
yes, that appeals to some.
How often you used to fool me with that face
of pure, restful welcome—

then, if I leaned against you, I'd feel the sleet
of your look, go numb at your blast

of contempt, turn to a snow-wife of hate.
And we know, don't we, the last

of your roles? Remember, my dear, I played it with you
for long, bountiful seasons?
We bathed, we melted down to the bone in the blue
air, the ripe suns

of ourselves, stretched and vined together all over,
it seemed, sweltered, grew
lush undergrowth, weeds, flowers, groundcover.
I played and played with you,

day after burning day, the part of our lives
truest, perhaps, best,
and still can play it briefly if someone believes
I can: the sensualist.

Your cheek used to cool first and then re-warm,
but now our hot coinciding
is rare. Is this wordy drizzle a late-summer storm
or an autumnal? I'm hiding

something that wants to scream out, "Wait! Not yet!
It's too soon for me
to go away into thin air," a thing that
I can't say or see.

I see it, foolish and clear, and say it. Sometimes,
our minds are so used to whirling,
it's hard to believe the simple meters and rhymes
and explanations. Darling,

my world, my senses' home, familiar monster,
it would seem that I still love you,
and, like a schoolgirl deep in her first despair,
I hate to go above you.

PEONY STALKS

Peony stalks come up like red asparagus,
I said; my friend said they look like dogs' penises.
It was something misplaced I noticed, the color of a wound,
but she's right, it has something to do with love too in my mind.

In the peony bed in spring they bloody the ground.
Things go wrong. My neighbor goes mad. My dog is poisoned.
Last night I was told of a woman who dug seventy worms
daily to feed an unnested robin. One dreams

of these hard salvations. Yet now the robin returns
in the afternoon for his worms, and beats at the screens
in the evening to get to his perch in the cellar. They are wounded,
woman and bird are wounded. There is no end.

Who's found the proper place for love? I worry about you,
and about the uncared-for. There is a leak in my life now.
I watch a puppy chasing lightning bugs or butterflies,
plunging upward, and up, and up again, and besides he's

a sick puppy. Against intention, the feelings raise
a whole heavy self, panting and clumsy, into these
contortions. We live in waste. I don't know about you,
but I live in the feelings, they direct the contortions of the day,

and that is to live in waste. What we must do, we do,
don't we, and learn, in love and art, to see
that the peony stalks are red, and learn to say this
in the calm voice of our famous helplessness.

A GOODBYE

Getting a grip on the leash,
I shoot out the door
and am jerked down the steps
into leaf-mottled light,
so I'm a sudden hot-head,
or the world throws its wet
regrets onto my own
eyeballs. One after another
an animal whose need
I celebrate
calls me to the door.
I come, and he takes me out.

We have to go out.
One was churlish and rough
and died young.
Another was sweet and slow,
and came to my bedroom
in the middle of the night to say
that being loved helps,
but is not quite enough,
the worst thing he, poisoned,
ever told me, but it was true.
The present wit and rogue
leads me with gusto.

He trots me around the block
with skinned-knee boys
who talk big
and steer him home by the tail.
I wouldn't get near them
without him. I'd miss as well
the tonguelashing of her
whose Burning Bush he must douse
faithfully, night and morning,
and I wouldn't need to assure

frail ladies and shocked kittens
he's harmless, though immature.

Into their skin, these hounds,
I insert me,
and I go round-eyed
and ready-nosed, sniffing
sweated earth, air.
One instant judgment can bring
me blessings. But in the bounty
of these late afternoons I see
a shadow, reaching toward
the sidewalk, lengthening, too long,
till the sun itself
is furious and wrong.

My neighbor called
to tell me her cat was burned,
who jumped in a smoldering
garbage pit, and all furred
suffering I fear,
I see those gold paws charred.
I set my fearful hand
on the leash of my friends
and am led into this hard
sensibility, over and over,
and over and over
a shadowed word. . . .

But look.
I turned this corner
with a dog and a cat
and here you are,
my done-for humans,
standing together,
though you never met,
not in a merciful

disguise of metaphor,
but as yourselves.
I have been walking
away from you all year
in poem, letter,
talk and book.
You have become
terrible to me,
my dear and my dear.

After the long dying
and the sudden one,
when the calls struck
I began to run then,
to pretend I had never
seen you, but nothing
under the sun
could save me from slamming
into the eyes of your partners
where you kept on dying.
Snared in that place
where you were, were not, were,
I fell on my
frozen face.

I wanted to write you both
a good poem some day
with a line
long and strong
as our feeling for each other,
which broke
as our lives did
until the forms
again groped together
to admit what I have to admit,
that we go on uttering
our hopeless sing-song,

but like your funny salads,
your pauses on the phone,
and your wry, joky
self-disdain,
it will never come.
I can say it this way
to you because among
dapple of shade and sunshine
you loved me: the cat
has my mourning tongue.

MIDAS AND WIFE

He loved the way her fingers loved the ground,
a peasant touch that patted things green,
and would tent to petition for the rain

that made their garden move, and reach freely
for bugs that burrowed or birds that flew away.
She loved his gift for making that fairness stay.

But, lest she stay, he couldn't touch the queen
in whose cold image creation could be undone.
He feared his fingers and their golden gain,

but followed her from room to room
to touch what she touched. She arranged a trembling bloom,
he touched; the flower fell into its form.

The dog quivered and smiled at her attention,
but felt his brilliant answer and soon
froze forever in a witty grin.

The years went by, and all she carried inside
to feel his sovereignty, acquiesced and died
into perfection, and into the eternal married

except herself. The heart of Midas grew cold
from his abstention, the queen grew old,
and the whole palace filled with scions of gold.

She spoke then: "Look at my face, Midas, my shame
shouts to you there of my long affair with time
while I yearned for the king whose art could keep me home.

I reach for you through the world, and you never come,
you reach for what I touch, not what I am,
and down between us falls your golden theme.

Besides, I have grown so fond of the rich and still,
though all outdoors rage with the green and fruitful
I cannot bear my own composure until

you hold me. Changing under your touch, I'll prove
whatever holds perfectly is stronger than love,
but subject still to love's artless imperative.

Never on earth, my dear, can you and I
discover a golden mediocrity.
The sovereign gift must find a way to comply."

When Midas moved in loneliness and pain
to touch her hand, her hand turned numb,
her heart turned quietly into a paradigm,

and she took her final form in idolatry.
Blinding, and blind to him, her sun-like eye,
but her brazen lips could move him anyway,

and Dionysus, smiling, set him free.

TWO POEMS FOR SUB-ZERO TIMES

I

Who says the world is mud? For the fifth day
the snow holds hard and white and cold birds
cross-stitch their search for seeds on all its edges.
To crack and smoke for a while is a winter decision.
My dog and the neighbors' dogs have wetted gold,
loops and chains of gold around the trees
and dabbles of gold where men can't smell out the reason.

Who says that man is mad? It is my joy
that walks behind this animal and watches
him urinating flowers and necklaces.

II

*"Remember: the most beautiful woman in the world is made of the very
same chemicals as you."*
                    Advertisement for a book by Gaylord Hauser

Winter has stiffened the ground, the birds are gone,
the air is still and clear, all branches refuse
to break their crystal coats for some supple gesture.
Today the Sunday paper brings me news.

It tells me my silly salts and vinegars
wish for destruction, cause me to enjoy
thoughts of hot and riotous consummations,
of bridges burning, and the town a Troy.

But tells me, till love's nucleic acid fleshes
that churning idiot of a Helen inside,
to wash my face in kitchen herbs and simples,
to eat my yoghurt, and be satisfied.

ECONOMICS

Out of a government grant to poets, I paid
to be flung through the sky from St. Louis to San Francisco,
and paid for tours and cruises and bars, and paid
for plays and picnics and film and gifts and the ho-

tel for two weeks, and all the niceties
of sea, field and vineyard, and imports potted
and pickled and sugared and dried, and handouts for Hippies,
and walking shoes and cable and cab, and, sated

with wild black blare, Brahms, marimba and Musak,
and beaches, and cityscapes, uphill, downhill,
and colors of water, oil, neon, acrylic,
and coffees spiced, spiked, blazing, cool,

foamed, thick, clear, on the last night,
two extra suitcases packed to go home again,
with the last of the travellers' checks paid for eight
poets to dine with me in Chinatown:

hour after hour of rich imagery,
waiters and carts, delights of ceremony,
fire of sauce, shaped intricacy
of noodle and dumpling, the chicken cracked from clay,

its belly crammed with water chestnut and clam,
the shrimp and squid and lobster, the sweet and sour,
beer chill, broth and tea steam,
the great glazed fish coiled on its platter,

the chopped, the chunky, the salty, the meat, the wit,
the custard of almond and mint, the ginger cream,
the eloquent repletion I paid for——And yet,
did I spend enough in that city all that time

of my country's money, my country's right or wrong,
to keep one spoonful of its fire from eating
one hangnail, say, of one Viet Cong?

Don't clear the fish away yet," one poet said.
The cheek of the fish is a great delicacy."
With a spoon handle he probed away in its head
and brought out a piece of white flesh the size of a pea.

"For the hostess," he said, "from all her grateful gourmets."
In SAVE THE CHILDREN ads I've seen the babies.
Filled with nothing but gas and sour juice,
their bellies bulge like rotten cabbages.

"One dollar to CARE will pay for ninety meals."
They cry. They starve. They're waiting. They are in anguish.
How can we bear to imagine how it feels?
Pain. *Pain.* I ate the cheek of the fish.

In an instant of succulence my hideous maw
swallowed, I'd guess, the dinners of fifty children.
What good does it do to really take that in,
and what good does it do to vomit it out again?

Gentle reader, should I economize?
I write poems for fifty cents a line.
This poem is worth what it's worth to the families
of two human beings under the age of eighteen

to see them blown to pieces. "Indemnification
for civilian casualties: from eight dollars
and forty cents for a wounded child, on
up to the top sum of thirty-three dollars

and sixty cents for a dead adult." I tipped
the waiter fifteen percent, which came to nine dollars.

Economics

The cab drive was a third of a child. I slept
each night for a fourth of his mother. What are dollars?

And what are words, as formed and plump on the page
as Chinese dumplings? Or love, that mink stole,
that sweepstakes prize for one in a million? What wage
could I ever earn that would let me afford to feel

how a newborn, somewhere, is learning to focus
on a world that drains its pus in his eyes like an eyesore?
Our right to see the beauties of this world grant us
that we may grant it, or
                              Christ, what are poems for?

"TO RECORD ONE MUST BE UNWARY"

This wet morning a seasonal
joke's been played on my lawn.
Several dozen scrolls
of sycamore bark, thrown
by someone divesting himself
of a whole year's news at once,
lie there again.
Somewhere among them is *my* newspaper,
rolled in its rainproof tan.

How silly one feels, hunting
for the sense of one day ago
among statements that a year has ended.
Yet how much does a tree know?
Like me, very little, no doubt.
We've both had experience, though:
in breeze, the engagement of foliage,
in gale, the numbing crack
of heart, or elbow—

—but one musn't be sentimental.
I know I'm more like a Russian
than a tree is like me; to be
"incapable of locomotion"
makes one more innocent,
limits one's aggression,
defines one as a plant,
and dooms one to feel, but not fool with,
the agonies of fission.

Besides, I'd rather resemble,
not this sycamore, but someone
frugal. Guarded. Encrusted.
Someone whose stance (someone,
oh Lord, who has *learned* something)
as he waits for another year

of war and weather to begin
is not this soft, iridescent, indecent
standing in his underskin.

Ah, but through my sapwood
a natural stupidity
rises, sometimes, with such sweetness
that what I want to say
is leaf, not leaflet. I believe,
then, that it's nice to be tree,
a big, blind, blameless
character who takes the air
unconsideringly.

I guess it's as well that whoever
has been teased by metaphor
should see me like this, in the open,
wholly unable to compare
or to choose between the reports,
confounded by a sycamore;
should watch me going gray
from white no-news of this morning
and black news of mornings before.

THE TALKER

One person present steps on his pedal of speech
and, like a faulty drinking fountain, it spurts
all over the room in facts and puns and jokes,
on books, on people, on politics, on sports,

on everything. Two or three others, gathered
to chat, must bear his unending monologue
between their impatient heads like a giant buzz
of a giant fly, or magnanimous bullfrog

croaking for all the frogs in the world. Amid
the screech of traffic or in a hubbub crowd
he climbs the decibels toward some glorious view.
I think he only loves himself out loud.

WEST BRANCH PONDS, KOKADJO, MAINE

Where hundreds of frogs
cluck like a couple of frantic hens, each a first-time mother,
I have come in my character.

I step over burned pizzas
dropped among blooms by the lone cow,
admire with a downward glance, dutifully see,
heal-all and bunchberry,
try not to sneeze at vistas
of hawkweed, Joepyeweed, yarrow.

The meaning of this, once, I will enter,
albeit through burning gates of hayfever
and a failure to make or to seize
the useful categories.

I enter, peeling, bobbing on top, grim,
the cookpot of the trout pond, with its scalloped,
smoky rim.
Now we are all together in the stew:
one moose stuffed with waterlilies, you,
five flyfishers,
two mergansers and I.
Slowly the round fire
comes down from on high,
the sky turns to a cover,
the water begins to simmer, then *ppt, ppt, ppt,*
with nosing trout,
to bubble all over.

Am I more hardboiled, or more tender
after half an hour?

Next time, I row toward a young male moose,
wasting my film from far off

(I can't believe he's learned to be tame).
I try to look in his eyes
and keep crooning, "Good boy, come,
I wouldn't hurt you, nice boy, nice . . ."
He lets me get to fifteen feet from his rough,
wet chest, and then, toward home,
I back off as fast as my fear can row me.

How foolish the fear. He was used to posing
and knew me as soon as he saw me.

Still further back in the woods a campcook has fed
the birds all summer,
and I look . . . the campers and I only look in our need.
Who ever saw before a gold or a purple finch
light on a human shoulder?
Well, they know which side of their lunch
is suet-and-peanut-buttered.

And, marvelling, I try to remember
that they'll fly away before the camp is closed
and it gets unaccountably, unbelievably
colder.

There aren't any poisonous snakes in the state of Maine.
The watersnake at the spring,
a shy half-foot of telephone wire,
is in retreat when I come with my jug,
and comes back when I've finished its filling.
But didn't I come to become aware
of something? Of something bigger?
Oh Serpent, in what alderthicket are you hiding?
Or leering from the limb of what jackpine?
It seemed so simple.

I only wished to be worldly like you,
to be as supple.

West Branch Ponds, Kokadjo, Maine

My knowledge? From the heart
it comes in a hiss.
The myth of the garden was beautiful and clear,
but it withered before I loved and hurt.
Lord of the fallen world, it is
my innocence that is the evil here.

THE CITIES OF THE PLAIN

Their sex life was their own business,
I thought, and took some of the pressure off women,
who were treated, most of the time, as merely
a man's way of producing another man.
And there were plenty of the other kind—
the two older girls got married when they wanted to.
The riot in front of our house that evening,
when a gang of young queers, all drunk and horny,
threatened to break in, yelling
for the two strangers, our guests, handsome
as angels, to come out and have some fun,
was not intelligently handled by my husband,
to say the least. An uptight man,
he got so frightened he opened the door
and offered to send out our youngest girls
if they'd quiet down and leave us alone.
"Two little virgins," he told them. "Now, fellows,
wouldn't that be nicer, and more fun?"
That made them wild, and they would have dragged
him out and mounted him in the street
if our guests hadn't managed to get the door shut.

The two strangers, it turned out, were Inspectors.
Don't ask me why, for the sake of a Perfect
Idea, of Love or of Human Community,
all the innocent-eyed, babies and beasts
and birds, all growth, both food and flower,
two whole cities, their fabulous bouquets
of persons, frivolous, severe, rollicking,
wry, witty, plain, lusty,
provident, every single miracle of life
on the whole plain should be exploded
to ashes. I looked back, and that's what I saw.

Nobody knows my name. My husband
and our two adolescents kept their faces

turned to the future, fled to the future.
Sarah everyone knows, whose life,
past menopause, into the withered nineties
was one long, obsessed attempt to get pregnant,
to establish the future. As for me, I lost
all sense of human possibility
when the cloud rose up like a blossom over all that
death. I stood for nameless women
whose sense of loss is not statistical,
stood for a while, then vanished. Men
are always being turned to stone by something,
and loom through the ages in some stony
sense of things they were shocked into.
I was not easily shocked, but that punishment
was blasphemous, impiety
to the world as it is, things as they are.
I turned to pure mourning, which ends the personal
life, then quietly comes to its own end.
Each time the clouds came and it rained,
salt tears flowed from my whole being,
and when that testimony was over
grass began to grow on the plain.

A SMALL EXCURSION

Take a trip with me
through the towns in Missouri.
Feel naming in all its joy
as we go through Braggadocio, Barks, Kidder, Fair Play,
Bourbon, Bean Lake
and Loose Creek.
If we should get lost
we could spend the night at
Lutesville, Brinktown, Excello, Nodaway,
Humansville or Kinderpost.

If we liked Bachelor we could bypass
with only slight compunction
another interesting place,
Conception Junction.

I think you would feel instant intimacy
with all the little flaws
of an Elmer, Esther, Ethel, Oscar or Archie,
all the quirky ways
of a Eunice or a Bernice,
at home in a
Hattie or even an Amazonia.

I'd enjoy, wouldn't you, saying that I came from
Chloride, or Map or Boss or Turtle
Or Arab or Chamois or Huzzah or Drum.

Surely the whole world loves the lover of men
who calls a tiny gathering
in midwest America
Paris, Carthage or Alexandria,
Odessa, Cairo, Arcadia or Milan,
as well as the one who calls
his clump of folk

Postoak,
the literalist who aims low
and calls it Shortbend or Old Mines
or Windyville or Iron or Nobby or Gumbo.

Riding along together,
we could think of all we'd had
at both Blooming Rose and Evening Shade.
Heading into the setting sun,
the gravel roads might get long and rough,
but we could make the difficult choice between
Minimum and Enough,
between Protem and Longrun.
And if it got very late
we could stay at Stet.

Isn't there something infinitely appealing
in the candor
of calling a collection of human beings
Liberal, Clever, Bland, or
Moody, Useful, Handy, or
Rich, Fertile and Fairdealing?
People who named these towns
were nobody's fools.
Passing through Peculiar, we could follow
a real school bus labelled Peculiar Public Schools.

O to be physically and aesthetically
footloose,
travelling always,
going through
pure sound that stands for a space,
like Cabool, Canalou, Plad, Auxvasse,
Koshkonong, Weaubleau, Roubidoux,
Hahn Dongola, Knob Noster and Foose!

SINCE YOU ASKED ME. . . .

For the sweet sake of inscapes
don't be afraid to plead—
in fashion even plaid
does, for pattern, and now goes with
both flowers and stripes.
It may even be myth
that before a fall pride goeth.
Be proud to be outrageous
so long as you have an almost religious
regard for un-with-it truth.
If you want to, stick with rhyme;
that linguistic sunbeam
says things are, and are not, the same
as they were last year,
and I'm sure
that, accidental or intentional,
or external or internal, or both,
it does not, at least, represent sloth.
All of us feel losses, but we
were robbed, not of "the pastoral dream of youth"
so much as the pastoral dream of maturity.
Poets over forty, start to fight.
To write
"in mockery of system"
is the ultimate slavery
to system, of all things! Why rhyme?
To say I love you to language, especially now
that its only viable components seem to be
"like," "y'know?" and "Wow!",
to tickle the ear of those with musical savvy,
to break down the distinction between light verse and heavy,
to say that human ingenuity
can walk hand in hand with responsibility.
It's a challenge to chaos *hurled*.
Why use it? Why, simply
to save the world.

And why use measure? That linguistic sundial
is not just style but lifestyle,
telling us, *pace* Hamlet,
that after all—I'll say it forever, damn it—
life in the harsh world's worthwhile.
But don't write those little tiny
poems like "THE", centered on a blank page.
Even Henny-Penny,
when she thought the sky was falling,
considered it a more important outrage
than might be expressed in a poem like "Feeling/
tired by the midnight
of
it
all/I

went to bed."
Surely, given mind and senses, there's more to be said.

WITH WARM REGARDS TO
MISS MOORE AND MR. RANSOM

When life, love, poems
begin to need horseradish,
one begins to wonder who was responsible for that waggish
invention.
The wheel dazzles, but I wish
there were clues to the imaginative journey
by which something deep, and with difficulty dug up, was led
from gross root to dish.
The first bite must have made a man cry out
for a drink of water,
yet he clung to the notion of eating it
to the extent of trying a grater
and then some vinegar and some salt, and even then
the amount to dabble on something, and on what
to dabble it must have taken
a good deal of thought.

No nourishment was involved there,
though most people must have been searching through nature
for something more filling than
"only consonants and vowels."
But perhaps the old theory preserved it, that
if it's bad enough
it must be some kind of cure.
One can imagine, certainly, the outraged howls
of someone who chewed it on someone's advice
for a direct benefit,
to restore virility, say, or loosen the bowels.
And they gave it
that name because it was obviously more suited
to a horse's coarse palate
than to any man's, and yet
when they learned how to diffuse its not very humane
flavor, that was the moment
their culture received a definite advancement:
art in its aspect of pure enhancement.

The idea of horseradish,
like random rhymes in the verse of a poet
who'd enjoy feeding rhymes to the reader's ear
as if they were
the minced worms and saliva Lorenz' pet jackdaw,
who mistook him for a fair
lady daw, poked down that open orifice,
but who knows it is the fashion to diet,
fascinates me
sometimes obsessively.
The thinking reed thought of a weed
that tasted like poison,
like the desert sun
that takes from the body more than it gives,
as nevertheless a sunshine,
wanted to pick its seed and sow it,
to save what horseradish is.

Value. How to define that.
Whatever helps some?
After while in a jar horseradish will become
only a sour mush with a mild tang.
I think of a wedding ring
and of the green life in a limb
which slowly, quietly, imperceptibly withdraws
until again
the startle of a fresh spring noon
sends new juices spurting down the stem.
Like orgasm, which is like pain,
(and you can't live on orgasm, you won't live on pain)
you don't take it plain,
you thank the man who discovered horseradish,
yield to what he must have been thinking of,
and spread it with care over the solids of the day
like married love.

END OF MAY

Atop each stem
an iris or two has turned in
on itself with no regrets and given up
color. Pink, yellow and red,
the rosepetals are spread
so wide they already tend
toward total drop.
Peony litter covers the ground.
On earlier days
friends and neighbors in pairs have been summoned
to have a drink and see the bloom,
have admired everything and gone.

I sit in my suntan oil alone—
almost alone—a jay
tries to flap me away
from his drinking trough.
His coarse, demanding rebukes
pierce my ears. He chirks
news of impending drouth.

But under my feet as I tan
is no longer a brick patio,
rather a light brown
paisley made of seed wings
from the silver maple, which can sow
faster than I can sew
this fine fabric into something.
And in the air,
like a great snow,
are flakes alive with purpose.
The cottonwood huffs and puffs
them everywhere.

On oil that sheathes me from sun
they cling to bare parts of person.

End of May

All the long, late
day, my arms and legs are furred
with such a will to beget
I think I can almost afford
to forget it's only skin-deep.
It's like taking dope.

It's too late, I tell the tree,
you've settled on somebody seedless.
Equivocally, it nods its head.
But I have been overheard.
Maybe for you but not for me,
the seedy old world says.

EVENING STROLL IN THE SUBURBS

The night is uneasy, armed between streetlamps.
Gaslights watch, dusk-to-dawn, for the sneak.
A footfall brings raging dogs from their porches.
Thorned shrubs replace flowerbeds, and stumps
where walked dogs used to take a leak
are planted round with unkind cactus.
Murmur and rustle of lovers, sibilance
of a lone bike, jolly ker-slaps
of a jogger are stilled. Each front lawn,
which formerly proffered the elegance
of a poised rabbit, poisoned its slopes
with DDT. Fear is overgrown.
The corner drugstore's boarded, For Rent.
Somewhere out here the hater, the thief,
the hurter, the disturber of peace must be.
In this barbed neighborhood, oh I want
back the self that night-walked, safe
from screaming in the dark, It's only me.

WHAT THE MOTORCYCLE SAID

Br-r-r-am-m-m, rackety-am-m, OM, *Am:*
All—r-r-room, r-r-ram, ala-bas-ter—
Am, the world's my oyster.

I hate plastic, wear it black and slick,
hate hardhats, wear one on my head,
that's what the motorcycle said.

Passed phonies in Fords, knocked down billboards, landed
on the other side of The Gap, and Whee,
bypassed history.

When I was born (The Past), baby knew best.
They shook when I bawled, took Freud's path,
threw away their wrath.

R-r-rackety-am-m, *Am*. War, rhyme,
soap, meat, marriage, the Phantom Jet
are shit, and like that.

Hate pompousness, punishment, patience, am into Love,
hate middle-class moneymakers, live on Dad,
that's what the motorcycle said.

Br-r-r-am-m-m. It's Nowsville, man. Passed Oldies, Uglies,
Straighties, Honkies. I'll never be
mean, tired or unsexy.

Passed cigarette suckers, souses, mother-fuckers,
losers, went back to Nature and found
how to get VD, stoned.

Passed a cow, too fast to hear her moo, "*I* rolled
our leaves of grass into one ball.
I am the grassy All."

Br-r-r-am-m-m, rackety-am-m, OM, *Am:*
All—gr-r-rin, oooohgah, gl-l-utton—
Am, the world's my smilebutton.

A VIEW

You drive, the road aims for a mountain.
Down paving, toward the low basket of the sun,

a jackrabbit is dribbled by slaps of hot wind.
Hummocky, glazed, superficial, tanned

the landspread. I ride beside you, in the time
of life to note character, waiting for the sublime.

Enhancement of hills. Foisted up by their trite
avowals, we grow more close and hot.

Far ahead, something definite is about to occur.
The way goes flat, dusky. There they are,

the god, looming, and with him—but she is terrible!—
lying at his feet, his own foothill,

wrinkled, blue, balding, risen-above,
her back all sore from trails, child-ridden, shoved

to the ground in a dumpy heap, mined-out,
learned-on by the high one until that

moment he knew his own destiny, donned
a green-black cloak, rose up around

mid-life to stay with the stars, his face flint,
his eyes slatey and bland, and she went

into her change. Oh she was fanciful once,
garbed in dapples of yarrow, lupine and gentians,

silvery inside, always a-chatter
with rockchuck and nuthatch, point-breasted, and later

glad to be taken. Opened unmercifully,
she was used all over. Then, so accessible, she

was fair game for everyone. Even her shale
surfaces have been wrung out for oil.

He stands nearby, unmoved. He knows
how not to be. Even at sundown he flourishes.

He can sway in aspen and tender seedgrass
in his low meadows, wearing the disgrace

of his early delicacy still, where blue grouse,
calliope hummingbird, rosy finch rise

and fall in paintbrush, harebell, penstemon,
beeplant, columbine. Nothing is gone.

He shows without shame these young, soft
traces, having gone on to lift

into view rock ribs and evergreen
masculinity. He transcends every mine,

they are small scars in his potency, something
unearthly shocked, shook him and kept him ascending.

He grew rough, scrabbly, wore outlaw underbrush,
gray fox, bobcat and cougar, secret fish.

Then he was stale for a while, all bare bone, then reared
a feast of self in a head uncovered,

streaked gray and white, playing cool, leaning
on no shoulder, above raining,

oblivious of his past, in pride of escape.
Never down-hearted, he is wholly grown up.

You turn and ask how I am. I say
I'm admiring the scenery, and am O.K.

WALKING THE DOG: A DIATRIBE

I have never seen a cicada, but nothing so pollutes
the night with noise as those self-absorbed, ear-baiting singers,
even in the night of a big wind, not the blurbs
of trees, shaking and shouting their leaves at each other,
not the girlish swish of tires on a street distorted to highway,
nor, in gusts, all the clattery trash set out at curbs;
there is nothing so loud, not the *Boo! Wawboooo!* of a coon-
    hound,
whose throat, shaped for sounding the hunt through miles of
    thicket,
is leashed to the suburbs.

They are being natural, the cicadas. Need more be said?
And the eye, that must take its delight, what weather then is this
for its succoring stroll? Hound and I walk in a gross
distortion of shapes and shadows which lunge in the light-and-
    black
of night and storm and one streetlamp. Too close to the sidewalk,
plantings of pyracantha spread an emboss,
over their mean thorns, of elaborate foliage and berries.
What do they know of what is insufferable
in their ignorant gloss?

Yet they lash as we linger to take in the violent evening.
Back home, my skin crawls with the sense that I've been through
    something.
Woven between hedges and treerows there are, even in wind-
    storms,
strings of light tension I broke, and I brush at the invisible
felt facts of my journey, I feel for the invisible makers,
hoping to finger webs, threads, spiders, worms.
How do I know what I've done, how does anyone know
what breakthrough or heartbreak has been accomplished in a dark
where there are no forms?

LETTERS FROM
A FATHER
AND OTHER POEMS
1982

LAST

LETTERS FROM A FATHER

I

Ulcerated tooth keeps me awake, there is
such pain, would have to go to the hospital to have
it pulled or would bleed to death from the blood thinners,
but can't leave Mother, she falls and forgets her salve
and her tranquilizers, her ankles swell so and her bowels
are so bad, she almost had a stoppage and sometimes
what she passes is green as grass. There are big holes
in my thigh where my leg brace buckles the size of dimes.
My head pounds from the high pressure. It is awful
not to be able to get out, and I fell in the bathroom
and the girl could hardly get me up at all.
Sure thought my back was broken, it will be next time.
Prostate is bad and heart has given out,
feel bloated after supper. Have made my peace
because am just plain done for and have no doubt
that the Lord will come any day with my release.
You say you enjoy your feeder, I don't see why
you want to spend good money on grain for birds
and you say you have a hundred sparrows, I'd buy
poison and get rid of their diseases and turds.

II

We enjoyed your visit, it was nice of you to bring
the feeder but a terrible waste of your money
for that big bag of feed since we won't be living
more than a few weeks longer. We can see
them good from where we sit, big ones and little ones
but you know when I farmed I used to like to hunt
and we had many a good meal from pigeons
and quail and pheasant but these birds won't
be good for nothing and are dirty to have so near
the house. Mother likes the redbirds though.
My bad knee is so sore and I can't hardly hear
and Mother says she is hoarse from yelling but I know
it's too late for a hearing aid. I belch up all the time

and have a sour mouth and of course with my heart
it's no use to go to a doctor. Mother is the same.
Has a scab she thinks is going to turn to a wart.

III

The birds are eating and fighting, Ha! Ha! All shapes
and colors and sizes coming out of our woods
but we don't know what they are. Your Mother hopes
you can send us a kind of book that tells about birds.
There is one the folks called snowbirds, they eat on the ground,
we had the girl sprinkle extra there, but say,
they eat something awful. I sent the girl to town
to buy some more feed, she had to go anyway.

IV

Almost called you on the telephone
but it costs so much to call thought better write.
Say, the funniest thing is happening, one
day we had so many birds and they fight
and get excited at their feed you know
and it's really something to watch and two or three
flew right at us and crashed into our window
and bang, poor little things knocked themselves silly.
They come to after while on the ground and flew away.
And they been doing that. We felt awful
and didn't know what to do but the other day
a lady from our Church drove out to call
and a little bird knocked itself out while she sat
and she brought it in her hands right into the house,
it looked like dead. It had a kind of hat
of feathers sticking up on its head, kind of rose
or pinky color, don't know what it was,
and I petted it and it come to life right there
in her hands and she took it out and it flew. She says
they think the window is the sky on a fair
day, she feeds birds too but hasn't got
so many. She says to hang strips of aluminum foil

in the window so we'll do that. She raved about
our birds. P.S. The book just come in the mail.

v

Say, that book is sure good, I study
in it every day and enjoy our birds.
Some of them I can't identify
for sure, I guess they're females, the Latin words
I just skip over. Bet you'd never guess
the sparrows I've got here, House Sparrows you wrote,
but I have Fox Sparrows, Song Sparrows, Vesper Sparrows,
Pine Woods and Tree and Chipping and White Throat
and White Crowned Sparrows. I have six Cardinals,
three pairs, they come at early morning and night,
the males at the feeder and on the ground the females.
Juncos, maybe 25, they fight
for the ground, that's what they used to call snowbirds. I miss
the Bluebirds since the weather warmed. Their breast
is the color of a good ripe muskmelon. Tufted Titmouse
is sort of blue with a little tiny crest.
And I have Flicker and Red-Bellied and Red-
Headed Woodpeckers, you would die laughing
to see Red-Bellied, he hangs on with his head
flat on the board, his tail braced up under,
wing out. And Dickcissel and Ruby Crowned Kinglet
and Nuthatch stands on his head and Veery on top
the color of a bird dog and Hermit Thrush with spot
on breast, Blue Jay so funny, he will hop
right on the backs of the other birds to get the grain.
We bought some sunflower seeds just for him.
And Purple Finch I bet you never seen,
color of a watermelon, sits on the rim
of the feeder with his streaky wife, and the squirrels,
you know, they are cute too, they sit tall
and eat with their little hands, they eat bucketfuls.
I pulled my own tooth, it didn't bleed at all.

V I

It's sure a surprise how well Mother is doing,
she forgets her laxative but bowels move fine.
Now that windows are open she says our birds sing
all day. The girl took a Book of Knowledge on loan
from the library and I am reading up
on the habits of birds, did you know some males have three
wives, some migrate some don't. I am going to keep
feeding all spring, maybe summer, you can see
they expect it. Will need thistle seed for Goldfinch and Pine
Siskin next winter. Some folks are going to come see us
from Church, some bird watchers, pretty soon.
They have birds in town but nothing to equal this.

So the world woos its children back for an evening kiss.

LIVES OF THE POETS

I was fortunate enough to have
a mother who on one occasion
encouraged me by commissioning
a poem. Newly married, I
was tackling my first teaching job
when a letter came which said, in part:
"As writing is so easy for you
I want you to write a poem about
the San Benito Ladies Auxiliary
that I belong to. Our club has twenty
members and we bake cute cookies
and serve them with coffee and do our sewing
at the meeting. We make stuffed animals
to give poor Texas kids at Xmas.
We meet on every other Wednesday.
Tell all that in the poem. Write
the poem to be sung to the tune
of Silent Night Holy Night
as that is the only song I have learned
to play so far on my accordion.
I want to play and sing it at
the club meeting. I could do it myself
of course but writing makes me nervous.
I'm sure you will do this for me because
it is so easy for you and I know
you wouldn't want me to get nervous.
I have to have it this week so I
can get it down pat for the next meeting."

In the midst of grading a hundred or so
freshman themes, trying to master
A Vision so I could teach Yeats, and reading
the output of my creative writing
class, I wrote the poem for her.
(Some of the rhymes were hard.) I'm only
sorry that I didn't keep
a copy, and that I missed the performance.

SPEAK, MEMORY!*

For once she gets to go with big Cousin Beatie,
who is starting her breasts. They're at Uncle Charlie's farm.
Grandma says, "Ach, Kind, what will they think of next
enahow, the town school? Hunt the butterflies, yet!"
But Beatie says, "It's an *Assignment*."

Mother says, "Now *go*, first." But she hates the outhouse,
where you have to close yourself in with the awful stink
or the collie will try to lick you while you sit on the hole.
Aunt Cora has made two nets from wire and cheesecloth,
and they each take a net and a canning jar.

"How many kinds of butterflies are there, Beatie?"
"I don't know. I have to make a *Collection*."
They're on flowers. "Where are some flowers, Beatie?"
(Mother has beds of bachelor buttons and cosmos.)
"Along there." "Where?" "Right *there*, dumbbell."

Between the road and the cornfield (now she can see)
humps of dust and sand turn to black-eyed Susans,
thistle, goldenrod, clover. And a little white flutter.
"There's one! Run!" Down and out of the ditch,
thrashing through scratchy weeds. Run!

It zigs to the cornfield, lifts overhead. "Oh, shoot!"
They walk and walk. The sun burns down. The cornfields
rustle beside them. A car goes bumping by,
throwing clouds of stinging dust over their sweat.
There. A white one. Run! "I *got* him!"

The sun burns. "These are all the same,
let's look in the pasture." They hold the bob-wire for each
    other.

* This poem refers to, and partly depends upon, for its similarities and
its ironic contrasts, another version of a writer's childhood—Vladimir
Nabokov's in Speak, Memory!

Gnats fly up and stick on her wet skin.
"There's some more white ones." Run! She trips over burdock,
slips on cow-pies. "*I* got one!"

(Where are the black-striped big ones she's seen at home?)
It's hard to breathe. The sun pounds on her head.
Itch-bumps and dirt mottle her arms and legs.
Devil's pitchforks pock her anklets. Hummocks trip her.
Grasshoppers rattle up in her face.

The red-and-white cows munch and mourn, but won't hurt you.
Sweat runs under wet bangs and into eyes.
They sit in the shade of a tree for a while. "My butterflies
got sort of broken." "There's some more white ones." Run!
(Mother won't like the rip in her bloomers.)

"We better go home." "How many we got?" "Seven,
but they're all the same." "Well, one of 'em's almost yellow."
"Heck, there ain't any other kind around here. I'll flunk
my *Assignment*." "Gee!" Her feet fall into road ruts,
she burns and chills all the way back.

Through the back yard where the hens huddle in dust holes,
around the slimy white mud where dishwater's thrown,
through swarms of flies at the door, and into the house
with its flies, its faint, strawy smell of cow manure,
its kerosene lamps and Congoleum flowers.

The parrot is calling the dogs in Aunt Cora's voice,
"Here Rover, here Sport!" and whistling them "wheet, wheet,
    wheet,"
(Mother calls her cockers Togo and Peewee)
and the silly farm dogs are coming on a panting run.
It's nearly time for bread-and-milk supper.

Grandma says, "Gott in Himmel, look the poor Kinder!"
They pump pee-colored rainwater to cool their faces
at the tin-lined sink. Cleopatra, Oak Eggars, Tortoiseshell,
Speckled Woods, Eupthecia nabokovi,
where were you that hot day in Iowa?

GROWING UP ASKEW

They had the Boston Bull before I was born,
and Mother liked her far more than she liked me.
We both had a trick. When Mother shaved one forefinger
with the other and said, "Shame, *sha-a-me!*" Peewee
would growl and snap most amusingly right on cue.
I, when shamed in the same manner, would cry.
I see my error now, but what good does it do?

PHOTOGRAPHS

"Take what you want, we'll throw the rest away.
The mice are building nests in the box, we don't
want that old stuff anymore." My father, 88,
kicks the box over to me with his good leg.
My mother sits on her pee-damp paper pad,
trying to take part. The box is jammed to the top
with photos and albums, dust and chewed-up rug wool.
I dump and sort. Their parents' wedding pictures
scorched on cardboard where dimly and patiently
they held their breaths and posed for the sulphurous flash—
the men perched rigid in wicker studio chairs,
the girls standing beside in long, dark,
serviceable, handsewn gowns, their faces
stiff and startled as a dahlia presented
in a frill of ruching or of tatted lace,
one hand on the husband's shoulder, where it stayed.
Then with their broods of children, young, half-grown,
grown, their faces turning stern, parental,
bodies swelling, then melting down. "Surely
you want this batch." My parents shake their heads.
They are nobody's children now, or mine perhaps.

Their brothers and sisters, the fat, self-righteous face
of Grace, the missionary, who told me, eight
years old, "You're a bad, *bad* girl to say 'my goodness.'
Do you know why?" "No." "Because Goodness is GOD!"
May, the educated one, capped, gowned,
adopted by a rich and childless aunt
and given "advantages." Brought back for dinner
once with her own siblings, she laughed and cried out,
pointing at Dad, "Look at that boy's big nose!"—
a story my father told with bitterness
till he was in his sixties. Cora, whose faith-healer
couldn't cure the cancer she hid from her doctor.
Brownie, whose beautiful dark eyes were closed
to near-blindness by their drooping lids when she fell

downstairs and struck her head as a young bride.
Al, lover of poop-pillows, plastic turds
and pop-up snakes, whose youthful high-jinks
twisted to drunkenness and kleptomania.
The others, too, outlived. "I'll take all these."
Their web of love and hate has been broomed away.

"Who's this young woman?" My mother holds the picture
up to her eyes and squints her best. Dad takes it.
"Oh, *I* know, Anna Meinberg, Mother's chum.
When I was courting I always had to bring
a man for Anna or Mother wouldn't go."
He laughs toward Mother, but she doesn't smile.
"Throw it away." They are not lovers now.

I sort in the dimming light. My mother dozes.
'Who are all these children, Dad?" "Must be
your mother's folks, some Richsmeier or Peters kids."
They sit patiently, brushed, told to hold still,
their legs in black stockings and feet in high-top shoes
stuck out in front of them, the button-eyed
babies in crocheted caps with ribbon pom-poms
on either ear, sacked in tucked gowns or naked
like rubber dolls, their faces plump possibility.
For all three of us, they go in a discard pile.

And now a precious stack, my parents themselves:
The boy with his plowing team, the young father
with pompadour, the deep family lines
already scored between brows. ("When I grow up
I'm going to marry Daddy!" Then Mother's jealous
"Well you can't. *I* married him." "Why can't
I marry him too?" "Because you *can't*, that's why!")
Posed proudly with his bantams, with his turkeys,
goats (he never lost his farmer's heart).
Small eyes that never saw another's pain
or point of view ("Your mother's always complaining.

I've fed and clothed her all her life. What more
does she *want?*") Full lips that laid down the law for us.
Big feeder before his heart attack, his Santa
belly swells in the gas station uniform.
"You'll have to feed him good," his mother told
his bride. "If dinner's late just hurry and set
the table. He'll think the food is almost ready."
Pride in the stances. "My word's my bond. I've never
cheated man nor woman." Pride of place:
"All that education will make you Big-Headed."
"All that reading will make you lose your mind."
My mother, the youngest, the beauty of her clan,
minx who wooed big brother Al away
from Cora, his twin, and held him clutched lifelong
in mischief and complicity. Expressive
face I studied all my childhood to learn
if I was wrong or right, kept or cast out.
Best cook in town, best seamstress—not enough.
"I'd have been a great singer if I hadn't married."
"I could have been a nurse if I hadn't had you."
In a ruffled dustcap, her arms and lap piled full
of eleven puppies, then standing with a braid
of thick hair down to her knees, then bobbed, marcelled,
then permed—the lovely features never show
her "nerves," the long years of dissatisfaction,
the walks she took me on when I reached adolescence
and poured my hard ear full of my father's failings.
"Don't tell *me* about it, it's not my fault,
I didn't marry him!" "Mother, wake up.
I wish you could see this picture of your long hair."
"I could *sit* on my hair." The old boast comes by rote.
"You want to keep this batch a little longer, don't you?"
"No." Those faces have turned fictional.

And now their only child, long-legged, skinny
from trying to please and hardly ever pleasing.
Long curls my mother wound on rags for a while,

then highschool ugliness, then a fragile gauze
of beauty young womanhood laid on the lens, then lifted,
with my young husband slowly changing beside me,
my father's face stamped clearer and clearer on mine,
sterile publicity pictures, graying hair.
I need not ask the two frail watchers my question.
They are no longer parents. Their child is old.

The last's my ace—my father's great adventure.
Suddenly he bought a housetrailer and pulled
his startled family from our Iowa village,
out of the cornfields and into the world's wonders,
all the way to Washington, then down
the California coast, then back to home,
packing a trunk so full of memories
they've lasted him for nearly fifty years.
The earth erupted for us all in moonscapes
of Black Hills, mountaintops hung from the sky
(the old Pontiac boiling on every pass),
Salt Lake held you up without an inner tube,
rodeos bucked in Wyoming, bears rocked the trailer
at night in National Parks, great waterfalls roared,
Mother and I made snowballs in July
on Crater Lake and posed before studios
in Hollywood, we all stood on Boulder Dam,
our fan belt broke in the desert and Dad hitchhiked
while I fainted from the heat. On the desert, too,
in the one hundred twenty degree trailer, Mother
boiled potatoes and made gravy for dinner.
"If I don't get my spuds every noon I'll drive
us right back home!" We knew he meant what he said.
For years we all re-lived the trip, Dad using
the album to remind himself of stories,
used it to entertain any company—
old friends, then new ones elsewhere—then, years later,
the hired help of their old age. Still later
I'd use it to get him going, to cheer him up,

to distract him from worries, boredom, aches and pains.
I turn on the light. "Dad, here's our *trip!* Remember. . . ."
He interrupts, staring at the darkened window,
"Everything's rusting away out in the garage.
It's been so long since I could get outside . . ."
My mother stirs. "When's the girl going to fix
my banana and coffee? I want to go back to bed."
I close the box. Somewhere a telephone
has made the appointment—a flower-scented pose
where they wait with patience for one witnessing heart
to snap its picture of their final faces.

THE STREAM

for my mother

Four days with you, my father three months dead.
You can't tell months from years, but you feel sad,

and you hate the nursing home. I've arranged a lunch
for the two of us, and somehow you manage to pinch

the pin from Madrid I bought you closed at the neck
of your best red blouse, put on new slacks, and take

off your crocheted slippers to put on shiny shoes,
all by yourself. "I don't see how you could close

that pin. You look so nice!" "Well, I tried and tried,
and worked till I got it. They didn't come," you said.

"Mother, I'm sorry, this is the wrong day,
our lunch is tomorrow. Here's a big kiss anyway

for dressing up for me. The nurse will come in
tomorrow and help you put on your clothes and pin."

"These last few days her mind has certainly cleared.
Of course the memory's gone," your doctor said.

Next day they bathed you, fixed your hair and dressed
you up again, got a wheelchair and wheeled you past

the fat happy babbler of nonsense who rolled her chair
all day in the hall, the silent stroller who wore

a farmer's cap and bib overalls with rows
of safety pins on the bib, rooms of old babies

in cribs, past the dining hall, on down to a sunny
lounge in the other wing. "Where can I pee,

if I have to pee? I don't like it here, I'm afraid.
Where's my room? I'm going to faint," you said.

But they came with the lunch and card table and chairs
and bustled and soothed you and you forgot the fears

and began to eat. The white tablecloth, the separate
plate for salad, the silvery little coffee pot,

the covers for dishes must have made you feel
you were in a restaurant again after all

those shut-in years. (Dad would never spend the money,
but long ago you loved to eat out with me.)

You cleaned your soup bowl and dishes, one by one,
and kept saying, "This is fun! This is *fun!*"

The cake fell from your trembly fork, so I fed
it to you. "Do you want mine, too?" "Yes," you said,

"and I'll drink your milk if you don't want it." (You'd
lost twelve pounds already by refusing your food.)

I wheeled you back. "Well, I never did *that* before!
Thank you, Jane." "We'll do it again." "Way down *there*,"

you marveled. You thanked me twice more. My eyes were wet.
"You're welcome, Mother. You'll have a good nap now, I'll
    bet."

I arranged for your old companion, who came twice a day,
to bring you milkshakes, and reached the end of my stay.

On the last night I helped you undress. Flat dugs
like antimacassars lay on your chest, your legs

and arms beetle-thin swung from the swollen belly
(the body no more misshapen, no stranger to see,

after all, at the end than at the beloved beginning).
You chose your flowered nightgown as most becoming.

You stood at the dresser, put your teeth away,
washed your face, smoothed on Oil of Olay,

then Avon night cream, then put Vicks in your nose,
then lay on the bed. I sat beside your knees

to say goodbye for a month. "You know I'll call
every Sunday and write a lot. Try to eat well—"

Tears stopped my voice. With a girl's grace you sat up
and, as if you'd done it lifelong, reached out to cup

my face in both your hands, and, as easily
as if you'd said it lifelong, you said, "Don't cry,

don't cry. You'll never know how much I love you."
I kissed you and left, crying. It felt true.

I forgot to tell them that you always sneaked your meat,
you'd bragged, to the man who ate beside you. One night

at home, my heart ringing with what you'd said,
then morning, when the phone rang to say you were dead.

I see your loving look wherever I go.
What is love? Truly I do not know.

Sometimes, perhaps, instead of a great sea,
it is a narrow stream running urgently

far below ground, held down by rocky layers,
the deeds of mother and father, helpless sooth-sayers

of how our life is to be, weighted by clay,
the dense pressure of thwarted needs, the replay

of old misreadings, by hundreds of feet of soil,
the gifts and wounds of the genes, the short or tall

shape of our possibilities, seeking
and seeking a way to the top, while above, running

and stumbling this way and that on the clueless ground,
another seeker clutches a dowsing-wand

which bends, then lifts, dips, then straightens, everywhere,
saying to the dowser, it is there, it is not there,

and the untaught dowser believes, does not believe,
and finally simply stands on the ground above,

till a sliver of stream finds a crack and makes its way,
slowly, too slowly, through rock and earth and clay.

Here at my feet I see, after sixty years,
the welling water—to which I add these tears.

THE CASE OF THE

Drinking the seconal dissolved in bourbon,
stabbed in the fog, shoved into quicksand,
caught in the telescopic sight,
feeling a sudden pressure on the carotids from behind,

scalped, buried, bombed, smothered in cellophane,
"another blow and another, savage, fast,
unreasoning," in Amsterdam,
Gary, Indonesia, Alabama, Budapest,

perilous, perilous the keeping of the human spirit.
Killed everywhere, on the train, in the tomb,
generosity, at the racetrack, grace,
at the tiller, down the sewers, in the unguarded hospital room,

willingness, in the London slum, on the plane,
at the mountain resort, strength, in the pew,
on Golden Gate Bridge, affection. Nowhere to hide.
Everywhere, everywhere someone is out looking for you.

One, with his mouth hung open to hear,
grunts "Huh?" after every statement. "*Huh?*"
His prostate swells, blood pressure bangs his head.
"This country's gone to the dogs and the hippies can go too."

And one pees fourteen times a night,
missing the bedpan every other time.
Her false teeth clicking with malice, she whispers,
"If you don't watch them every minute they'll *steal you blind.*"

Are the passersby in collusion? Did the victim
deserve what he got? The search for evidence
goes on and on, the light burns,
the sirens whine, the long report says you only live once.

Fingerprints, autopsies, exhumations
tell us a great deal, but the shoes
don't fit anyone we know. As for the bodies,
some were fair of face, some had nothing to lose.

On the last page, the one-eyed witness,
trapped by the D.A., drops his dreams and his lies,
his squirrel mouth opens, and he squeals all he knows:
"The sun done it, coming up every damn morning like it does!"

THERE

IN THE MISSOURI OZARKS

Under an overwashed, stiff, gray
sheet of sky, the hills
lie like a litter of woodchucks,
their backs mottled black with leafless
branches and brown with oakleaves,
hanging on till spring.
Little towns are scabs in their haunches.

Out of the hills the pickups scuttle
like water beetles onto the highway,
which offers up STUCKEY'S, EATS,
GOD'S WELL, CAVES,
JUNQUE, HOT BISCUITS 'N'
CREAM GRAVY, $6. OVERNIGHT
CABINS and a WINERY
to the chilled traveller.

Town leads off with a garish motel,
followed by the Shopping Plaza—
a monster of a supermarket
and a few frail shops; then comes
the courthouse square, with a barnfaced
Dollar Department Store,
Happy's Hardware and TV,
Shorty's Beer-Cafe,
two quiet banks and a chiropractor.
Big white gingerbreaded houses
and new ranchstyles
fizzle out on the edge of town
to yellow, brickpatterned tarpaper
shacks, leaning against the firewood
stacked as high as their roofs.

Off the highway, frosty weeds
lift berries and pods
on either side of the road in a mileslong

wine and black and beige bouquet,
and every twenty acres or so
a fieldstone cottage
guards its pastured cows
and its woods of oak and black walnut.
Farm dogs explode from porches
and harry the car down the gravel,
yipping at stones spat from the wheels.
Out here, after the supper dishes,
three or four couples will walk down the road
to a neighbor's, and will sit
around the heating stove,
talking about Emma Harbis,
who is finally giving away cuttings
of her famous orange-blooming
Kalanchoë, and about the Ed Lelands,
on food stamps all year,
but with a brand new pickup
parked bold as brass
in their front yard, and about
Old Lady Kerner, who was seen
in the drugstore buying Oil of Olay
to smooth out the wrinkles
eighty-two hard years have hammered
into her indomitable face.

MOOSE IN THE MORNING, NORTHERN MAINE

At six A.M. the log cabins
nose an immense cow-pie of mist
that lies on the lake.
Nineteen pale goldfinches perch
side by side on the telephone wire
that runs to shore,
and under them the camp cow,
her bones pointing this way and that,
is collapsed like a badly-constructed
pup tent in the dark weeds.
Inside, I am building a fire
in the old woodstove with its rod overhead
for hunters' clothes to steam on.
I am hunting for nothing—
perhaps the three cold pencils
that lie on the table like kindling
could go in to start the logs.
I remember Ted Weiss saying,
"At the exhibition I suddenly realized
Picasso had to re-make everything he laid his eyes on
into an art object.
He couldn't let the world alone.
Since then I don't write every morning."

The world is warming and lightening
and mist on the pond
dissolves into bundles and ribbons.
At the end of my dock there comes clear,
bared by the gentle burning,
a monstrous hulk with thorny head,
up to his chest in the water,
mist wreathing round him.
Grander and grander grows the sun
until he gleams, his brown coat
glistens, the great rack,
five feet wide, throws sparks

of light. A ton of monarch,
munching, he stands spotlit.
Then slowly, gravely, the great neck lowers
head and forty pounds of horn
to sip the lake.
The sun stains the belittled
cow's hide amber.
She heaves her bones and bag
and her neckbell gongs
as she gets to her feet
in yellow blooms of squaw-weed.
On the telephone wire
all the little golden bells are ringing
as that compulsive old scribbler, the universe,
jots down another day.

THE HERMIT OF HUDSON POND

"Like most of the hermits in the area
[he] obeyed to the letter the Fish and Game Laws."

In the "immaculately neat" cabin it is calm and warm.
Deermice with Disney ears run the rafters by day
and rustle, gnaw and squeak in the provisions at night.
The snowshoe rabbit, red in sun as a setter,
hops and sits, twitching its nose, outside the door,
and all around, from trees to ground, the air
flashes with the yellow and black and white flight
of Evening Grosbeaks, fat with the spruce budworms
they feed on. The pond, like a great pan of broth,
bubbles with feeding trout when the hatch comes on.
For forty years, the days dawn and darken
in quiet order for the hermit of Hudson Pond,
only one law reaching in to his natural place.
No women with their feverish voices and strange, bloody days,
nor men, murdering, hustling, re-making the world,
only the self trimmed to its simplest needs,
shelter, food, for friendship a dog, and the days
dawning and darkening on woods and pond,
the moose wading in, mergansers churning the water
like motorboats as they scoot for a fish, loon
hooting and yodeling, or, when the snow comes,
the deep, still white, the burning, glistering cold.

"June 9, 1961" the flying service pilot
checks on the hermit and finds a note in the cabin:

"I killed myself because I had to kill
my baby dog for chasing deer. I threw
my pistol into the lake after I shot
baby dog. I didn't have nerve enough
to shoot myself. I didn't have to shoot
my dog. No one knew she was chasing deer
but me. I want to suffer because I think

273

it was a crime to shoot my baby dog.
If you find this, Ray, I'm all done living. I'm on
the bottom of the lake beside my dog."

Quotes from Anne Howe, "Hermits of the Moosehead Region,"
MOOSEHEAD, MAINE BICENTENNIAL BOOKLET, 1976

MADRID, 1974

I

All the world is walking on the Gran Via,
we too, locked into step in the evening parade:
double-breasted businessmen in blocky trios,
slinky sweethearts, grandmas in black with faces like wintered-
over apples, longhairs humped by backpacks,
couples with the kids, the babybuggies and the perros.
Buildings along both sides are layer cakes
of light—from all levels alert leather shops,
doll shops, paella parlors, one-floor
hotels and beauty salons dangle with hope
their tiny, hard-to-find elevators.
The crowd compresses where cafe tables fly outdoors
and settle on the Avenida and where lines are forming
under marquees that translate "Deliverance" or "The Sting."
A stream of vowels that all the world shouts
flows over the pebblebacks of cars rolling down the center.
And yet, already, more than a block away
from our own cafe, where she locates herself, I can hear her,
AW-EE-AW (surely she has swallowed a foghorn), her bray,
above the honk and hubbub, the voice of a giantess
invoking chance in a strange language, the voice of my Muse.

II

At our home cafe we're sipping Schweppes limon.
Regulars here are having their pastry and coffee
(as regulars in bars in the Old Town
are having grilled shrimp, sausage, squid and wine,
and children in plazas are running with a sugar bun
in one hand, and teens at corner counters are gulping
their "hot little dogs.") It is eight o'clock. Dinner's at eleven.
Our local gigolo, with purse and cane,
sits with a hennaed matron, then with a bleached one.
Guitar-slung, our hippie hustles pesetas for a hostel.
Against the glass front our elegant shoe-shine
gentleman leans at ease. Our favorite sign

across the street lights up: EL EDEN DE LOS
  PANTALONES.
But it is she, our lottery lady, who gives life and tone
to the place. On other corners cripples and crones
whine and sell the touch of a wen or a humped back,
but she's square and light on her feet as a box of Corn Kix.
Wide bosom flapping with tickets, embodied luck,
she flirts at each table. They feed her forkfuls of cake.
She sweats, slaps at flies and smiles. She'll shoot out like a bee
at the passers, light on someone, and exchange a joke.
All the world laughs with her. When a table is empty
she'll scrub it dry with her hand out of sheer energy.
The waiters wink. Often she'll stand and yell,
voice aimed at the whole city, at farmer, at gypsy
in the mountains beyond: EE-AW, come to me and all will be
  well.

III
Four flights overhead they're cooking our half-pension meal.
How I love the cold crunch of Gazpacho, the wry red wine,
the shiny green and black olives and their oil,
the Huevos Flamenca, the tick of a fork on a seashell
in the saffron rice, the Sangria aswirl with sliced lemon
and apple, the sugary oranges, the musky sting
of the brandy! How I love, like a Spanish king,
El Greco, Goya, El Bosco, Zurburan,
the stagey Plaza Mayor, the swarming Puerta del Sol—
in fact, except for the corrida, everything, everything!
In the loteria of grants my number came up.
Skimming olivegroves spattered with poppies, the plane did not
  fall.
For more than a thousand days I have not been ill.
Some dear ones are still alive. The world is full,
and its servant, the word, through art's little ee-aw-ee,
praises its fullness in every lucky country.

MADRID, MAY, 1977

"Spain will surprise you." SUAREZ

Tooting down the Gran Via,
tossing out bundles of loose white leaflets,
the campaign caravans roll.
At nine in the evening
leaflets snow on the heads and shoulders
of Madrilenos at sidewalk cafes
and cover their plates of hot, fried churros,
while those in the paseo scuff through leaflets stained with
streetdust and churro grease.
Mornings, out of each porteria pops
a porter with broom like a jack-in-the-box
to bare his section of the street
for a few hours until the tooting begins
again, and the paper snow.
It is a serious carnival.

The waiter who speaks English
and looks like a sad prizefighter
sets down my plate of langostinos
and says, "Yes, we have learned
very quickly how to disagree.
The hardest thing we must learn now
is how to disagree without violence."

Off the main streets we walk in a city
of paper walls, one hundred
and fifty-nine parties have built these surfaces
of pasted paper and print.
Like bears on hind legs sharpening their claws,
men and women stand by the walls
and scratch with their fingernails
at the campaign posters they disagree with,
ripping tiny strips from the print.
We pass a five-year-old,
scraping with his nails at a poster.

Madrid, May, 1977

This is a new game.
Only people over sixty-two have
ever played it before.

In the evening stroll, young lovers in jeans,
twined together like churros,
writhe through double-breasted businessmen,
past posters of La Pasionaria,
past bare breasts blooming on news kiosks,
past movie lines for uncensored sex.
For good or ill, America strolls up the street.

At midnight, coming from supper,
we stop at a gray clump on the sidewalk.
It is a pile of puppies.
They are asleep,
cuddled together on the pavement
in a litter of leaflets.
Off to one side, their owner
dickers with three possible customers,
each of whom has for a moment forgotten
that, in a few weeks, having placed
a slip of paper in a plastic urn,
into his empty right hand will fall
responsibility for his own life
and a share of responsibility for the world.

GOYA'S "TWO OLD PEOPLE EATING SOUP"

It was gray.
There was no gruel
for hours, years.
All around me
drone of a
dead world.
Dry cold rocks
in my bed,
rocks of hours, years.
The skin sank
to the skeleton
and stuck,
dry.

Then
the steam of celery
soaked my face clean.
A lump of potato
lit
on the back of my tongue,
warm weight.
The stock
seeped into sockets
and soothed
my bones.
The onion
clawed open
my nose.
My eyes
consumed the bowl
whole.
The red beans
rolled under my gums
and the carrots were blazing
with life, with *life*.

AT PÈRE LACHAISE

What began as death's avenue
becomes, as we go on,
death's village, then metropolis,
and the four of us,
reading our rain-blistered Michelin
map of graves, keep looking back,
but cafés, tabacs,
boulangeries are gone.
It is a long way yet
to where we are going to please me,
and the bunch of muguets
I am holding too tightly is frayed
already. On either side
of the cobbles we slip on,
darkly arched over by dripping chestnuts,
the ten foot high deathhouses
stand, and we can see
at hilltop intersections
only further suburbs of
the imposing dead.
For a while we are lost
in this silent city—
the map is not detailed
and the avenues curve.
It is cold here. I am very cold.
My friend begins to cry.
We find a Kleenex for her
and a tranquilizer.
Head bent, hand clenched
to her mouth, her black bob
spattered with chestnut petals,
she stumbles and turns her ankle.
I am to blame.
A whole afternoon in Paris spent
on this spooky pilgrimage,
and we are too far in to go back.

The rain has stopped.
"Look, my God, *look!*"
Anything awful can happen here,
but I look where she points.
Ahead, at a break in the trees
where a weak ray of sun shines through,
two of the great dun tombs
are dappled with color, with cats,
more cats than I can believe,
two dozen at least,
sitting or lying on doorsills,
window ledges, pedestals, roofs,
and a yellow one, high in the air,
curled round at rest on the bar
of a towering cross.
Grimalkins, grandpas,
lithe rakes, plump dowagers,
princes, peasants, old warriors, hoydens,
gray, white, black, cream, orange,
spotted, striped and plain—
a complete society of cats,
posed while we stand and stare.
My heart is thumping.
"Are we dreaming?
Oh, aren't they beautiful!"
my friend whispers.
We smile at the cats for a long time
before we go on past.
We are almost there.

Off to the side,
behind the grand monuments,
we find a flat slab marked MARCEL PROUST
and, feeling a little foolish,
I lay my fistsized white bouquet
on his black marble.

At Père Lachaise

We go back another way
where the street widens,
opening out to gardens,
and we run down broad steps,
laughing at nothing.
A few people appear,
arranging gladioli in urns,
and far down the hill we can see
an exit to the boulevard.
We find Colette's grave
on the way out and call to her,
"You should have seen the cats!"

HERE

THE LEARNERS

We slapped the smirking mother
and the swollen father
and went to live in museums
and anthologies. Around us
were images of such fairness
that the world outside
was smoothed into smog.
We knew it was hard.
We were bony and strong
but our knuckles broke
as we cleaned and copied.

When rocks split the cellophane windows
we stumbled outside
leading the eldest.
Sun seared our eyeballs
and the cramp of the journey
crazed some of the seemliest.
Some of us dried to jerky.
When the light lowered a bit
some of us said they found
beauty beyond belief
in the ashes and oilspills.

When darkness came down
some mated, some murdered each other.
Some of us shook our fists
at the moon and the stars
for disdainful distance.
All over creation
there were sounds and shadows.
Digging into a cockpit of earth
with our broken knuckles
some of us sat and waited
with whatever was in the world.

RINGLING BROTHERS, BARNUM AND BAILEY

Thirty striped rumps in a circle with tails dangling.
One rump lifts and begins to dump, then spray.
At the crack of the cue, still pissing, she leaps to the ring
with the others and they all stand on their hind legs pawing
the air for balance. The dwarf on ten foot stilts
keeps stalking around the show, his little hands
waving, and we all wave every time round, and he tilts
to one side and staggers but now everybody is watching
the pony walk on his hind legs round and round
the kneeling camels while the whip flicks his strained belly.
Then, hanging by one wrist only, the aerialist spins
her whole body over . . . fifty times. "That's easy,
I could do that," the child behind me whines.
Directly overhead the tight rope walkers
work in a hush. (Three days from now one will smash
to her death in another town.) Absent watchers
are my two friends, one in the last months
of cancer, one in depression so deep she'll crash.
One leaps over the other. The rope holds. No one killed
today. "Anybody could do that. So what?"
the child whines, and I'd like to throw the child
and all brutal innocence under the elephant's foot.

CARING FOR SURFACES

Birds build but not I build, no, but wipe, Time's wife.
Dipped in detergent, dish and chandelier retrieve
their glister, sopped, kitchen floor reflowers, knife
rubbed with cork unrusts, colors of carpetweave
cuffed with shampooer and vacuum will reblush,
prints sprayed and scrubbed no longer peer but stare,
buffed, silver burns, brushed, plaster will gush
hue at you, tops soothed with cloth will clear.

Cleansing the cloud from windows, I let the world win.
It comes in, and its light and heat heave the house,
discolor, dim, darken my surfaces. Then once again,
as for forty years, my fingers must make them rouse.

Round rooms of surfaces I move, round board, books, bed.
Men carve, dig, break, plunge as I smooth, shine, spread.

CINDERELLA'S STORY

To tell you the truth, the shoe pinched.
I had no way of knowing, you see,
that I was the girl he'd dreamed of.
Imagination had always consoled me,
but I'd tried to use it with care.
My sisters, I'd always thought, were the family
romantics, expecting nice clothes to do the trick
instead of the beholder's transforming eye.
All that dancing I would have to have done,
if it *was* me, had made my feet swollen.
But I didn't know I'd been dancing, I thought him a dreamer.
He had everything—looks, loneliness,
the belief that comforting and love could cure
even an advanced neurosis.
I didn't know whether or not
he was deluded, but I was sure
he was brave. I wanted to have worn the slipper.

And that's all there was to the first transformation,
something that happened so fast I nearly lost it
with one disclaiming murmur, but something
that did happen, that he made me believe.

None of my skills but love was the slightest use
to my husband. Others did well at keeping
the home fires damped or hot.
And so I began to learn the sleeping
senses. I learned wholly to love
the man in the prince, what didn't dance:
bad breath in the morning, sexual clumsiness,
a childlike willingness to let the old queen
dominate. That was easy. And I read a lot.
Snarled in ideas, heading for the unseen,
I heard the wise men snicker when I spoke.
I learned that I had some beauty and, wearing
one gown or another for my husband's sake,

I learned of its very real enhancement.
That was a little harder. I had a ball
before I learned to use what beauty I had
with kindness and honor. That was hardest of all.
Our son was born, and I went to the child
through a clutter of nursemaids to tell him
how it feels to be poor. I started to grow old.
My husband saw everything and was grateful.
Thickening a bit at the waist, he firmed
and stayed, always, faithful.

And that was the second transformation,
slow and solid.
We were happy together.

Everything comes in three's, they say,
and I'm stuck in the third transformation,
flopping like a fish who's out of the life-saving
everyday water. I starve now for a ration
of dreams, I've never learned to live
without dreams. All through the filth and anger
of childhood I ate them like a calming sugar,
my sweet secret. I move through the palace,
gripping its ghostly furniture
till my fingers ache. I guess
that it is real, that I am living,
but what is there left to dream of?
I dream, day and night, of giving.

Prince, soon to be king,
we've made all our lovely exchanges
and my years as your princess are ending.
Couldn't there be, for me,
just one more fairytale?
More fiercely than the silliest clubwoman
in the kingdom, I try to hold onto my looks
because I dream that there was someone

warted, once upon a time,
waiting a kiss to tell him he too
could be beloved. My frog,
my frog, where shall I find you?

"There's something different about saleswomen in bakery shops.
They're happier, nicer." JARVIS THURSTON

SALESWOMEN IN BAKERY SHOPS

touch gently
with the tips of their
floured white fingers.

Round-faced and neat,
spry hair netted down,
they feel frosted with chocolate.

They move in a brightness
of raspberry,
in a warm flurry of
crust-flakes and ground almonds.

They smile with their apricot lips
and speak in a vanilla voice.
Radiance of ovens reflects on their cheeks.

They rest their eyes on
yeasty beds,
pillows of beaten eggwhite.
Lemon tingles
between their breasts.

Carefully, carefully they proffer
sugared shapes,
fragile twists,
soft sponge cups.

No sour returns
to scrape them,
no rape of goods.

Everything wild
is sweetened out of them.

Their tender transactions are finished
before the buttery dough
blotches the white sack
on the way home.

FALL

For James, who liked it

Here's that old drunk, already mellow.
A few nips and he's at his best.
Everything brightens up. Summer,
who can't stand him, gets somebody to take her
home. (She's spoiled and tired.) The rest
cluster around and enjoy his show.
Actually, they're the same jokes,
the one about the travelling mercury
and the farmer's pumpkins, the same tricks,
lighting bittersweet and sumac
without a match. Well, those who can't be
original can be good old boys.
A wall mural in lipstick, and he's back
at the bar. Now for those boozy tears,
you know they come from a cold will.
And now, for God's sake, one of his rages.
He's storming around, knocking down everything,
leaves, lovers, lights, stepping
on chrysanthemums. It seems ages
since he's been this bad. Then his brow clears
and he gives us his look: "Aren't I a smarty?"
Soon he'll pass out. Appalling! Still,
he's always welcome at the next party.

THE VISION TEST

My driver's license is lapsing and so I appear
in a roomful of waiting others and get in line.
I must master a lighted box of far or near,
a highway language of shape, squiggle and sign.
As the quarter-hours pass I watch the lady in charge
of the test, and think how patient, how slow, how nice
she is, a kindly priestess indeed, her large,
round face, her vanilla pudding, baked-apple-and-spice
face in continual smiles as she calls each "Dear"
and "Honey" and shows first-timers what to see.
She enjoys her job, how pleasant to be in her care
rather than brute little bureaucrat or saleslady.
I imagine her life as a tender placing of hands
on her children's hands as they come to grips with the rocks
and scissors of the world. The girl before me stands
in a glow of good feeling. I take my place at the box.
"And how are *you* this lovely morning, Dear?
A few little questions first. Your name?—Your age?—
Your profession?" "Poet." "What?" She didn't hear.
"Poet," I say loudly. The blank pink page
of her face is lifted to me. "*What?*" she says.
"POET," I yell, "P-O-E-T."
A moment's silence. "*Poet?*" she asks. "Yes."
Her pencil's still. She turns away from me
to the waiting crowd, tips back her head like a hen
drinking clotted milk, and her "Ha ha hee hee hee"
of hysterical laughter rings through the room. Again
"Oh, ha ha ha ha ha hee hee."
People stop chatting. A few titter. It's clear
I've told some marvelous joke they didn't quite catch.
She resettles her glasses, pulls herself together,
pats her waves. The others listen and watch.
"And what are we going to call the color of your hair?"
she asks me warily. Perhaps it's turned white
on the instant, or green is the color poets declare,
or perhaps I've merely made her distrust her sight.

"Up to now it's always been brown." Her pencil trembles,
then with an almost comically obvious show
of reluctance she lets me look in her box of symbols
for normal people who know where they want to go.

A WINTER'S TALE, BY A WIFE

Snorting hippopotamus at the lake's bottom, all snoot,
he lies against me, one arm clamping me down to the fate
he fell to after flying high all year unlit,
and over us, on eyelids, in ears, up noses, the steamer makes hot
waves of viral stew, the bed is marshy with flu-sweat.
Doomed, I thought, by his sneeze in my hair, no hypocrite,
nor amphibian either, I stayed snuggled night after night,
renouncing the cool beach of the guestroom bed, but felt hate.

Fiercer than usual, his passion, by a fake of fever, comes,
and his breath, through clogged airholes, must faster bubble and
   foam;
from head to toe my body, temperate, must take the
   unwholesome
smear of his leaking skin, while his huge achey limbs
jerk and lock toward ease, his sore-throat-bugs like gum
clump in my mouth. There's more to marriage than Freud
   could dream.
This dangerous stranger makes it new. My martyrdom
is romance. And he loves me that I do pity him?

Oh no—this hero fears his tragic isolation.
"Come wheeze with me," he thinks, "and like a pair of loons
we'll dive together to the undercover where all is one,
a murk of sameness. Separate, one sick, one well, we again
have to think of each other. A single handkerchief thickens
the plot, so let Kleenex be plucked by both and, clotful, be
   thrown
on both sides of the bed." But if I ail, my black lover's gone.
In a likeness of misery marital platters don't get licked clean.

And how, against his stuffed and swollen swoon, I feel
my lightness, neatness, sleekness of self, how cleanly, how cool
my voice issues from open sinuses! Let me stay well!
If his chest wheeze and purr, his m's turn to b's, my careful
enunciation, my resonance, will comfort, will fill

the fogged air with affectionate sympathy. Let me peel
for a good many more nights the gross from the ethereal,
lie thus lightly, less Caliban than before, more Ariel.

Besides, I get sicker than he does, cough longer, burn hotter,
    hurt more.
In the daytime I wield mops, pump legs, strain toward vigor,
make the dishwasher sterilize us apart, don't open my pores
before I go out, am lavish with Vitamin C (pure
nonsense). Oh the sweet breath that doesn't whistle in my clear
lungs! (It is by loving me that I know me, rather
than by knowing me that I love.) I bring him pills with sincere
concern, feed him and kiss him, but danger, danger is there.

Graying out of the sex culture, too bored to care who
can or can't have twenty-five bangs with a vibrator, you,
ma semblable, can thrill to think of lifting your husband's tissue
with spaghetti tongs. Proust, I thought, was a fantasist, since we
    do
not really invest each detail of our lives with such meaning,
    but now
he's justified, realist supreme—each snuffle I count to know
how close and closer I am to safety. I'll not get the flu,
I'll not—Ucchk—a tickle in my wrinkling throat? *Atchoo!*

In the old brownstone on W. 35th
death is the business,
"the contemplation of decomposing flesh
and smashed bone."
After a breakfast of brioches
with grilled ham and grape thyme jelly,
"the first shot, from behind, got his
shoulder and turned him around.
The second shot, from in front, got him
in the throat and broke his neck."
Lunch is seekh kebab, finished
with raspberries stirred in a
double-boiler mixture of cream, sugar,
egg yolks, sherry and almond extract,
then briefings of Saul, Fred and Orrie
for the tailings, the break-ins,
followed by anchovy fritters,
partridge in casserole
with no olives in the sauce, cucumber
mousse, and Creole curds and cream.
Stoked with Puerto Rican molasses
on buckwheat cakes, or eggs *au
beurre noir*, or corn fritters coated
with wild thyme honey from Greece,
or deviled grilled lamb kidneys,
Archie, the man of action,
goes out to view the corpse.
"The car knocked her flying for ten feet,
then, when she landed, speeded up
and rolled two of its wheels
over her body." He goes out
to get the facts,
returning to curried beef roll,
celery and cantaloupe salad
and blueberry grunt.
Eyes closed, pushing

his lips in and out, Nero Wolfe,
the man of intellect, thinks.
Verbatim reports. He said. She said.
"She was lying naked on the bed,
a silk scarf knotted around her neck.
Her face was no longer pretty."
Then mussel bisque, duck Mondor,
carottes Flamande and chestnut whip.
For Wolfe, from clams to cheese
is an hour and a half.
Interviews. Traps. Schemes. Fingerprints.
Parry and thrust with Inspector Cramer.
At 7 P.M. he goes to the diningroom
for sweetbreads *amandine* in patty shells,
cold green-corn pudding and rhubarb tart.
"At 11:07 P.M.
he was dead on the floor
with a statue on top of him."
Death is the business
in the old brownstone on W. 35th.

But in the kitchen, doing something with
artichokes, or, in his den
in the basement, dreaming over
294 cookbooks on eleven shelves,
Fritz, the real hero, holds up the house,
speaks, three times a day, for life.
"There will be shad roe, *en casserole*,
with anchovy butter. The sheets
of larding will be rubbed with five herbs.
With the cream to cover will be
an onion and three other herbs,
to be removed before serving."

FIRST

THE BALLAD OF BLOSSOM

The lake is known as West Branch Pond.
It is round as a soapstone griddle.
Ten log cabins nose its sand,
with a dining lodge in the middle.

Across the water Whitecap Mountain
darkens the summer sky,
and loons yodel and moose wade in,
and trout take the feathered fly.

At camp two friendly characters
live out their peaceful days
in the flowery clearing edged by firs
and a-buzz with bumble bees:

Alcott the dog, a charming fool
who sniffs out frog and snake
and in clumsy capering will fall
from docks into the lake,

and Blossom the cow, whose yield is vaunted
and who wears the womanly shape
of a yellow carton badly dented
in some shipping mishap,

with bulging sack appended below
where a full five gallons stream
to fill puffshells and make berries glow
in lakes of golden cream.

Her face is calm and purged of thought
when mornings she mows down fern
and buttercup and forget-me-not
and panties on the line.

Afternoons she lies in the shade
and chews over circumstance.
On Alcott nestled against her side
she bends a benevolent glance.

Vacationers climb Whitecap's side,
pick berries, bird-watch or swim.
Books are read and Brookies fried,
and the days pass like a dream.

But one evening campers collect on the shelf
of beach for a comic sight.
Blossom's been carried out of herself
by beams of pale moonlight.

Around the cabins she chases Alcott,
leaping a fallen log,
then through the shallows at awesome gait
she drives the astonished dog.

Her big bag bumps against her legs,
bounces and swings and sways.
Her tail flings into whirligigs
that would keep off flies for days.

Then Alcott collects himself and turns
and chases Blossom back,
then walks away as one who has learned
to take a more dignified tack.

Next all by herself she kicks up a melee.
Her udder shakes like a churn.
To watching campers it seems she really
intends to jump over the moon.

Then she chases the cook, who throws a broom
that flies between her horns,
and butts at the kitchen door for a home,
having forgotten barns.

Next morning the cow begins to moo.
The volume is astounding.
MOOOAWWW crosses the lake, and MAWWWW
from Whitecap comes rebounding.

Two cow moose in the lake lift heads,
their hides in sun like watered
silk, then scoot back into the woods,
their female nerves shattered.

MOOOAWWW! and in frightened blue and yellows
swallows and finches fly,
shaping in flocks like open umbrellas
wildly waved in the sky.

In boats the fisherman lash their poles
and catch themselves with their flies,
their timing spoiled by Blossom's bawls,
and trout refuse to rise.

MAWWOOOO! No one can think or read.
Such agony shakes the heart.
All morning Alcott hides in the woodshed.
At lunch, tempers are short.

A distant moo. Then silence. Some said
that boards were fitted in back
to hold her in, and Blossom was led
up a platform into the truck,

where she would bump and dip and soar
over many a rocky mile
to Greenville, which has a grocery store
as well as the nearest bull.

But the camp is worried. How many days
will the bellowing go on?
"I hope they leave her there," one says,
"until the heat is gone."

Birds criss-cross the sky with nowhere to go.
Suspense distorts the scene.
Alcott patrols on puzzled tiptoe.
It is late in the afternoon

when back she comes in the bumping truck
and steps down daintily,
a silent cow who refuses to look
anyone in the eye.

Nerves settle. A swarm of bumblebees
bends Blue-eyed grass for slaking.
A clink of pans from the kitchen says
the amorous undertaking

is happily concluded. Porches
hold pairs with books or drinks.
Resident squirrels resume their searches.
Alcott sits and thinks.

Beads of birds re-string themselves
along the telephone wire.
A young bull moose in velvet delves
in water near the shore.

Blossom lies like a crumpled sack
in blooms of chamomile.
Her gaze is inward. Her jaw is slack.
She might be said to smile.

At supper, laughter begins and ends,
for the mood is soft and shy.
One couple is seen to be holding hands
over wild raspberry pie.

Orange and gold flame Whitecap's peak
as the sun begins to set,
and anglers bend to the darkening lake
and bring up a flopping net.

When lamps go out and the moon lays light
on the lake like a great beachtowel,
Eros wings down to a fir to sit
and hoot* like a Long-eared owl.

* *The Long-eared owl's hoot resembles the whistle of tribute to the sight of something beautiful and sexy:* wheé *whée-you"*

Mona Van Duyn (Mrs. Jarvis Thurston) was born in Waterloo, Iowa in 1921 and since 1950 has lived in St. Louis. She has taught at the University of Iowa, the University of Louisville and Washington University, as well as at summer writing workshops: Breadloaf, Salzburg, Austria, in Texas, New York, Tennessee, Indiana and Maryland. With her husband she founded *Perspective, a Quarterly of Literature* (1947) and co-edited it until 1970. She has received The National Book Award (1971), The Bollingen Prize (1970) and The Pulitzer Prize (1991), as well as several prizes from *Poetry* including The Ruth Lilly Prize (1989) from that magazine and the American Council on the Arts. She was given a Guggenheim Fellowship in 1972. She is a member of the National Institute of Arts and Letters (1987) and a Chancellor of the Academy of American Poets (1985), having received its Fellowship in 1980. Washington University, Cornell College and the University of Northern Iowa have awarded her the degree of Honorary Doctor of Letters. In June of 1992 she was appointed by the Librarian of Congress as Poet Laureate Consultant in Poetry. A new book, *Firefall*, is published simultaneously with this one.

A NOTE ON THE TYPE

This book was set on the Linotype in Janson, a recutting made direct from type cast from matrices long thought to have been made by the Dutchman Anton Janson, who was a practicing type founder in Leipzig during the years 1668–1687. However, it has been conclusively demonstrated that these types are actually the work of Nicholas Kis (1650–1702), a Hungarian, who most probably learned his trade from the master Dutch type founder Dirk Voskens. The type is an excellent example of the influential and sturdy Dutch types that prevailed in England up to the time William Caslon (1692–1766) developed his own incomparable designs from them.

Printed and bound by Fairfield Graphics,
Fairfield, Pennsylvania